ANCIENT INDIA

PLATE I.

THE GIRNĀR ROCK IN 1869.

[See page 149.

ANCIENT INDIA

FROM THE EARLIEST TIMES
TO THE FIRST CENTURY A.D.

BY

E. J. RAPSON, M.A.

PROFESSOR OF SANSKRIT IN THE UNIVERSITY OF CAMBRIDGE AND FELLOW OF ST JOHN'S COLLEGE

WITH SIX ILLUSTRATIONS
AND TWO MAPS

GYAN

Published by

GYAN

Gyan Publishing House
5, Ansari Road
Daryaganj, New Delhi-110002
Phone: 011-47034999, 9811692060
E-mail: books@gyanbooks.com

Distribution Network
gyanbooks.com
India, USA, Canada, UK, Australia, France

ISBN : 978-81-212-3123-7 (PB)
First Published, 1916

2nd Impression 2020

Printed at: Gyan Press, Delhi.

Ancient India
Author: E. J. Rapson

ANCIENT INDIA

FROM THE EARLIEST TIMES
TO THE FIRST CENTURY A.D.

BY

E. J. RAPSON, M.A.

PROFESSOR OF SANSKRIT IN THE UNIVERSITY OF CAMBRIDGE
AND FELLOW OF ST JOHN'S COLLEGE

*WITH SIX ILLUSTRATIONS
AND TWO MAPS*

Cambridge:
at the University Press
1916

CAMBRIDGE UNIVERSITY PRESS

London: FETTER LANE, E.C.

C. F. CLAY, MANAGER

Edinburgh: 100 PRINCES STREET

Bombay, Calcutta and Madras: MACMILLAN AND CO., LTD.

Toronto: J. M. DENT & SONS, LTD.

Tokyo: THE MARUZEN-KABUSHIKI-KAISHA

PREFACE

In the following pages I have tried to write the story of Ancient India in a manner which shall be intelligible to all who take an interest in Modern India. My object has been to draw as clearly as possible the outlines of the history of the nations of India, so far as it has yet been recovered from the ancient literatures and monuments, and to sketch the salient features of the chief religious and social systems which flourished during the period between the date of the Rig-veda (about 1200 B.C.) and the first century A.D.

For the benefit of those who wish to continue the study I have added at the end of the book some notes on the ancient geography and a short bibliography of standard works.

In the transliteration of Sanskrit names I have followed a system which, while giving a strictly accurate representation of sounds, will, I trust, not puzzle readers who are not oriental scholars. If the vowels are pronounced as in Italian, with due attention to long and short (*e* and *o* being invariably long), the result will be sufficiently satisfactory for all practical purposes. Modern place-names are spelt as in the *Imperial Gazetteer of India* (new edition).

I am indebted to my friend, Dr F. W. Thomas, the Librarian of the India Office, for his kindness in obtaining for me permission to reproduce the illustrations, which are taken from negatives in the possession of the India Office.

To my wife, to Miss Mary Fyson, and to the Rev. C. Joppen, S.J., I owe my best thanks for much valuable assistance in reading proofs and in compiling the index.

E. J. RAPSON

ST JOHN'S COLLEGE
CAMBRIDGE
17*th February* 1914

CONTENTS

CHAP.		PAGE
I.	The Sources of the History of Ancient India	1
II.	The Civilizations of India	24
III.	The Period of the Vedas	36
IV.	The Period of the Brāhmaṇas and Upanishads	52
V.	The Rise of Jainism and Buddhism . .	64
VI.	The Indian Dominions of the Persian and Macedonian Empires	78
VII.	The Maurya Empire	99
VIII.	India after the Decline of the Maurya Empire	113
IX.	The Successors of Alexander the Great .	122
X.	Parthian and Scythian Invaders . . .	136
	Notes on the Illustrations	149
	Notes on the Ancient Geography of India	159
	Short Bibliography	176
	Outlines of Chronology	181
	Index	187

ILLUSTRATIONS

Plate I. The Girnār Rock in 1869 . . *Frontispiece*

Plate II. Coins of Ancient India . *Facing p.* 18

Plate III. The Besnagar Column . . . ,, 134

Plate IV. The Mathurā Lion-Capital . ,, 142

Plate V. Inscriptions on the Girnār Rock and on the Mathurā Lion-Capital . ,, 150

Plate VI. Inscriptions on the Besnagar Column ,, 157

MAPS

N.W. India and the adjacent Countries in the time of Alexander the Great *Between pp.* 78 *and* 79

The Principal Countries of Ancient India . *At the end*

ANCIENT INDIA

CHAPTER I

THE SOURCES OF THE HISTORY OF ANCIENT INDIA

The 'discovery' of Sanskrit—The Indo-European family of languages—The languages and literatures of Ancient India—Alphabets—Inscriptions and Coin-legends—Chronology—The rise of Jainism and Buddhism.

"THE *Sanscrit* language, whatever be its antiquity, is of a wonderful structure; more perfect than the Greek, more copious than the Latin, and more exquisitely refined than either: yet bearing to both of them a stronger affinity, both in the roots of verbs, and in the forms of grammar, than could possibly have been produced by accident; so strong indeed, that no philologer could examine them all without believing them to have sprung from *some common source*, which perhaps no longer exists. There is a similar reason, though not quite so forcible, for supposing that both the *Gothick* and the *Celtick*, though blended with a very different idiom, had the same origin with the

Sanscrit; and the old *Persian* might be added to the same family."

This pronouncement, made by Sir William Jones as President of the Asiatic Society of Bengal in the year 1786, may truly be called 'epoch-making,' for it marks the beginning of the historical and scientific study of languages.

At the time when Sir William Jones spoke these words, the recent discovery—or rather the recent revelation to Western eyes—of the existence in India of an ancient classical literature, written in a language showing the closest affinity to the classical languages of Ancient Greece and Rome, had raised a problem for which it was necessary to find some rational solution. How was the affinity of Sanskrit to Greek and Latin and other European languages to be explained? Scholars at the end of the eighteenth and the beginning of the nineteenth centuries were inclined to see in Sanskrit the parent language from which all the others were derived. It was only after the lapse of a generation that the view propounded by Sir William Jones began to prevail. The correctness of his conception of an Indo-European 'family of languages,' the members of which are related to each other as descendants of a common ancestor, has since been abundantly proved by the researches of Franz Bopp, "the founder of the science of Comparative Philology," whose first work was published in 1816, and by those of his numerous successors in the same field.

The science of Comparative Philology, which thus received its first impulse from the study of Sanskrit, represents by no means the least among the intellectual triumphs of the nineteenth century. The historical treatment of individual languages and dialects, and a comparison of the sound-changes which have taken place in each, have shown that human speech, like everything else in nature, obeys the laws of nature. The evidence obtained by this method proves that the process of change, by which varieties of language are produced from a parent stock, is not arbitrary, but that it takes place in accordance with certain ascertainable laws, the regularity of whose action is only disturbed by the fact that man is a reasoning and imitative being. The laws, which govern change in language, are, in fact, partly mechanical and partly psychological in character.

More valuable perhaps, from the point of view of the student of early civilization, is the service which Comparative Philology has rendered in throwing some light on the history of the Indo-European peoples before the age of written records. These peoples are found, in ancient times, widely scattered over the face of Asia and Europe from

Chinese Turkestān in the East to Ireland in the West; but, as we have seen, there must have been a period more or less remote when they were united. Now, since words preserve the record both of material objects and of ideas, it has been possible, from a careful examination and comparison of the vocabularies of the different languages, to gain some knowledge of the state of civilization, the social and political institutions, and the religious ideas of the Indo-European peoples, both at the period when they were still united and after the separation of the various branches.

In the earlier stages of the science, this line of investigation was, no doubt, sometimes pursued with too much zeal and too little discretion; and the evidence of language as a record of civilization was sometimes strained to prove more than was justifiable. But there can be no question that certain broad facts have thus been established beyond the possibility of dispute. The evidence of language proves conclusively, for instance, that a particularly intimate connexion must have existed between the Persian and Indian branches of the Indo-European family. The similarity in language and thought between their most ancient scriptures, the Persian Avesta and the Indian Rig-veda, can only be explained on the supposition that these two peoples, after leaving the rest of the family, had lived in association for some considerable period, and that the separation between them had taken place at no very distant period before the date of the earlier of the two records, the Rig-veda. In the following pages we shall be chiefly concerned with this particular group of the Indo-European family, which is usually designated by the term 'Aryan,' the name which both peoples apply to themselves (Avestan *Airya* = Sanskrit *Ārya*).

Such, then, were the first fruits of the study by Europeans of the classical language of Ancient India—a complete revolution in our conception of the nature of human speech, and the recovery from the past of some of the lost history of the peoples, who, in historical times, have played a predominant part in the civilization of both India and Europe. The 'discovery' of Sanskrit, with its patent resemblance to Greek and Latin, suggested the possibility of a connexion which was undreamt of before, and prepared the way for the application to languages of the historical and comparative method of investigation, which was destined to win its most signal triumph when it was applied subsequently by Charles Darwin and other great scientists to the material universe and to living organisms.

Familiar as the notions of an Indo-European

family of languages and of the scientific study of language may be to us at the present day, they proved a hard stumbling-block to all but the most advanced thinkers of the late eighteenth and the early nineteenth centuries; for they rudely disturbed the belief of many centuries past that Hebrew was the primitive language of mankind, and that the diversity of tongues on earth was the result of the divine punishment inflicted on the builders of the Tower of Babel.

But great and far-reaching as has been the influence of the 'discovery' of the Sanskrit language on the intellectual life of the West, no less remarkable are the results which have followed from the application of Western methods of scholarship to the interpretation and elucidation of the ancient literatures and monuments of India.

When, in 1784, the Asiatic Society of Bengal was founded by Sir William Jones for the promotion of Oriental learning, the history of India before the Muhammadan conquest in the eleventh century A.D. was a complete blank; that is to say, there was no event, no personality, no monument, no literary production, belonging to an earlier period, the date of which could be determined even approximately. A vast and varied ancient Sanskrit literature, both prose and verse, existed in the form of manuscripts; and European scholars, with the aid of the 'pandits' or learned men of India, were already beginning to publish texts and translations from the manuscripts. But as to the date of this literature nothing whatever was known. Sanskrit had ceased for many centuries past to be a language generally understood by the people. It had long since become, like Latin in the middle ages of European history, the exclusive possession of a class of learned men, who attributed to the sacred books a divine origin and regarded the secular literature as the work of sages in a dim and distant period of legend and mystery. The chronological conceptions of the pandits were those of the Purāṇas, which teach that the universe undergoes an endless series of creations and dissolutions corresponding to the days and nights of the god Brahmā, each of which equals 1000 'great periods' of 4,320,000 years. What we know as the historical period of the world was for them the 'Kali Age,' or the shortest and most degenerate of the four ages which together constitute a 'great period.' It was but as a drop in the ocean of time and might be neglected.

It is due almost entirely to the labours of scholars during the last century and a quarter that the outlines of the lost history of Ancient India have, in a great measure, been recovered, and that its literature, which reflects the course of religious and intellectual civilization in India from about 1200 B.C. onwards, has been classified chronologically.

The materials for the reconstruction of the history are supplied principally from three sources:—(1) the literatures of the Brahmans, Jains, and Buddhists; (2) inscriptions on stone or copper-plate, coins, and seals; and (3) the accounts of foreign writers, chiefly Greek, Latin, and Chinese.

At present, large gaps remain in the historical record and it is probable that some of them can never be filled, although very much may be expected from the progress of archæological investigation. Of the more primitive inhabitants of India we can know nothing beyond such general facts as may be gleaned from the study of prehistoric archæology or ethnology. History in the ordinary sense of the word, that is to say, a connected account of the course of events or of the progress of ideas, is dependent on the existence of a literature or of written documents of some description; and these are not to be found in India before the period when Aryan tribes invaded the country at its north-western frontier and brought with them an Indo-European civilization, resembling in its main features the ancient civilizations of Greece, Italy, and Germany. Our knowledge of Ancient India follows the course of this civilization as it spread, first from the Punjab into the great central plain of India, the country of the Ganges and the Jumna rivers, and thence subsequently into the Deccan. This extension is everywhere marked by the spread of Sanskrit and its dialects. It received a check in Southern India, where the older Dravidian civilization and languages remain predominant even to the present day. In this region history can scarcely be said to begin before the Christian era.

Thus, the language of all the earliest records of India, whether literary or inscriptional, is Indo-European in character. That is to say, it is related to Greek and Latin and to our own English tongue, and not to the earlier forms of speech which it supplanted in India. The Aryan tribes who continued, perhaps for generations or even for centuries, to swarm over the mountain passes into Southern Afghānistān and the Punjab, or through the plains of Baluchistān into Sind and the valley of the Indus, must, no doubt, have spoken a variety of kindred dialects. The history of languages everywhere shows that this is invariably the case among primitive peoples. It shows, too, that, in the course of time, when a community becomes settled and civilization advances, the dialect of some particular district, which has won special importance as a centre of religion, politics, or commerce, gradually acquires an ascendancy over the others and is eventually accepted by general consent as the standard language of educated people and of literature; and that, when its position is thus established, its use tends to supersede that of the other dialects. An illustration of this general rule may be taken from the history of our own language: it was "the East Midland" variety of the Mercian dialect of English "that finally prevailed over the rest, and was at last accepted as a standard, thus rising from the position of a dialect to be the language of the Empire" (Skeat, *English Dialects*, p. 66, in the series of Cambridge Manuals).

In India, such a standard or literary language appears first in the Hymns of the Rig-veda, the most ancient of which must probably date from a period at least 1200 years before the Christian era. This 'Vedic' Sanskrit is the language of priestly poets who lived in the region now known as Southern Afghānistān, the North-Western Frontier Province, and the Punjab; and it differs from the later 'Classical' Sanskrit rather more, perhaps, than the language of Chaucer differs from that of Shakespeare.

After the Vedic period, Aryan civilization

extended itself in a south-easterly direction over the fertile plains of the Jumna and Ganges, which became subsequently not only the chief political and religious centre of Brahmanism but also the birthplace of its rival religions, Jainism and Buddhism. It was in this region that the priestly treatises, known as 'Brāhmaṇas,' and the great epic poems, the Mahābhārata and the Rāmāyaṇa, were composed.

The language of each of these classes of literature—the Brāhmaṇas representing almost exclusively the priestly caste, the Brahmans, and the epic poems belonging chiefly to the warrior caste, the Kshatriyas—is, in a different sense, transitional between Vedic and Classical Sanskrit. In character, the two styles may broadly be distinguished as learned and popular respectively. The Sanskrit of the Brāhmaṇas merges in the course of time by almost insensible degrees into Classical Sanskrit; the epic language, on the other hand, is already stereotyped and retains its archaisms and its 'irregularities' for all time.

Thus, about the year 500 B.C., when the first work in strictly Classical Sanskrit appeared—Yāska's *Nirukta* or 'Explanation' of Vedic difficulties—there were in existence three well-defined types of Sanskrit. The first, already invested with a sacred character from its great antiquity, was the poetical language of the early Aryan settlers in the north-west. The second was the language of bards, who sang at royal courts of wars and the deeds of the heroes and sages of old time. The third, to which, strictly speaking, the term 'Sanskrit' (*saṃskṛita* = 'cultivated,' 'literary') should be confined, is that form of the language of the Brahmans, which, as the result of a long course of literary treatment and grammatical refinement, had gained general acceptance as the standard of correct speech.

A literary language thus definitely fixed ceases to undergo any material change, so long as the civilization which it represents continues. Its spoken form must naturally, as a rule, be less careful and elaborate than its written form; and both must vary according to the degree of cultivation possessed by each individual speaker or writer. There may thus be infinite varieties of style, but there is no substantial modification of the character of the language. Classical Sanskrit has remained essentially unaltered during the long period of nearly twenty-five centuries in which it has been employed, first as the language of the educated classes and of literature, and later, down to the present day, as the common means of communication between learned men in India.

In sharp contrast to the literary language of a country stand the local dialects. While the former is fixed, the latter still continue to have a life and growth of their own and to change in accordance with the laws of human speech. While the literary language, although no doubt originally the dialect of some particular district, gains currency throughout the whole country among the educated classes, the local dialects continue to be spoken by the common people, who, in Ancient as in Modern India, must have formed an overwhelmingly large proportion of the population. It is, therefore, chiefly by a perfectly natural process of development that most of the modern vernaculars of Northern India have been produced from the ancient local dialects or 'Prakrits,' as they are called (*prākṛita* = 'natural,' 'uncultivated'), in precisely the same way as the Romance languages have sprung, not from literary Latin, but from the dialects of Latin spoken by the common people.

While, however, the literary language and its dialects continue to exist side by side, the former invariably tends to grow at the expense of the latter, so long as the civilization to which they belong does not decline or change its character. The inscriptions and coin-legends of Ancient India afford a striking illustration of this fact. As being, from their very character, intended to appeal to all men, learned and unlearned alike, they are, on their first appearance in the third century B.C., written in some Prakrit; but, as time goes on, their language is gradually influenced and eventually assimilated by the literary language, until, after about the year 400 A.D., Prakrit ceases to be used for these purposes and Sanskrit takes its place.

The history of Sanskrit is especially associated with Brahmanism, and the tradition has remained through the ages unbroken by time or place. Sanskrit is to Brahmanism what Latin is to the Roman Catholic church. Jainism and Buddhism were revolts against Brahman tradition; and, like the reformed churches in Europe, both originally used the type of speech, whether Sanskrit or Prakrit, which happened to be current in the various districts to which their doctrines extended. Thus the Buddhist scriptures appear in a Sanskrit version in Nepāl and in Prakrit versions elsewhere. Through their employment for religious purposes some of the Prakrits developed into literary languages, for which, in the course of time, hard and fast laws were laid down by grammarians, precisely as in the case of Sanskrit. The most notable of these is Pali, the literary form of some Indian Prakrit which was transplanted to Ceylon, probably in the third century B.C., and became there the sacred language of the particular phase of Buddhism which found a permanent home in the island, and which has spread thence to Burma and Siam. In India itself, after about the fifth century A.D., there was a growing tendency on the part of both Jains and Buddhists to use Sanskrit, which thus eventually became the *lingua franca* of religion and learning throughout the whole continent.

Such then are the languages in which all the early literature of India and Ceylon is preserved. This literature is enormous in extent and most varied in character. No species of composition, whether in prose or verse, is unrepresented; and few phases of human intellectual activity remain without their record, except in the domain of those sciences, which have been, even in Europe, the creation of the last two hundred and fifty years. But, if we compare any ancient Indian literature, Brahman, Jain, or Buddhist, with the Greek and Latin classics, we shall find one striking deficiency; in none of them has the art of historical composition been developed beyond its earliest stages. Its sources—heroic poems, legendary chronicles, ancient genealogies—are indeed to be found in abundance. From the literatures and from the monuments we learn the names, and some of the achievements, of a great number of nations, who rose to power, flourished, and declined in the continent of India during the twenty-two centuries before the Muhammadan conquest; but not one of these nations has found its historian. Ancient India has no Herodotus or Thucydides, no Livy or Tacitus. Its literatures supply materials by means of which it is possible to trace the daily life of the people, their social systems, their religions, their progress in the arts and sciences, with a completeness which is unparalleled in antiquity; but events are rarely mentioned, and there is an almost total absence of chronology. Dynastic lists with, in some instances, the length of the different reigns, are certainly to be found; but these in themselves supply no fixed point for the determination of Indian chronology. As they stand, they are discrepant, partly perhaps because of original errors, but chiefly on account of the textual corruptions which are the inevitable result of a long transmission in manuscript form; and they are misleading, since they often represent as successive, dynasties which can be proved from other sources to have been contemporary. It has been shown that any system of Indian chronology, which could have been constructed on the data supplied by these documents alone, must have been hopelessly wrong by hundreds, and in some cases even by thousands, of years.

Fortunately, this defect in the literature is supplied to some extent from the other sources of early Indian History. For certain countries in India, and for certain periods in the history of these countries, it has been possible to construct a sort of chronological framework by the aid of dated inscriptions and coin-legends. This most valuable kind of historical evidence has been made available entirely by modern scholarship during the last three generations.

When the monuments of India first attracted the attention of archæologists, not a single syllable of the ancient inscriptions or coin-legends could be read. All knowledge of the ancient alphabets had, long centuries ago, passed into oblivion. These alphabets, which can now be read with ease and certainty, are two in number, both of them of non-Indian (Semitic) origin. They are called by scholars at the present time Brāhmī and Kharoshṭhī, the names which they seem to bear in an account of the youthful Buddha's education given in a Sanskrit work called the *Lalita-vistara.*

Brāhmī, which is usually, though not invariably (*v.* p. 151), written from left to right, has been shown to be the parent of all the modern alphabets of India, numerous and widely differing as these are now. It is probably derived from the type of Phœnician writing represented by the inscription on the Moabite stone (*c.* 890 B.C.) and it is supposed to have been brought into India through Mesopotamia by merchants. Ultimately, therefore, Brāhmī and all the modern Indian alphabets appear to have much the same origin as our own, since all the alphabets of Europe also are to be traced back to the Phœnician through the Greek.

Kharoshṭhī, which is particularly the alphabet of North-Western India (Afghānistān and the Punjab) is a variety of the Aramaic script which prevailed generally throughout Western Asia in the fifth century B.C. Originally, no doubt, it came from the same source as Brāhmī. Like most other Semitic alphabets, probably including Brāhmī in its earliest form, it is written from right to left. It disappeared from India in the third century A.D.; but it remained in use for some time longer in the western region of Chinese Turkestān, which had formed a part of the Indian Empire of Kanishka in the first century A.D.

The clue to the decipherment of both these alphabets was obtained from bilingual coins struck by the Greek princes who ruled over portions of Afghānistān and the Punjab from *c.* 200 B.C. to *c.* 25 B.C. These coins regularly bear on the *obverse* a Greek inscription giving the name and

PLATE II.

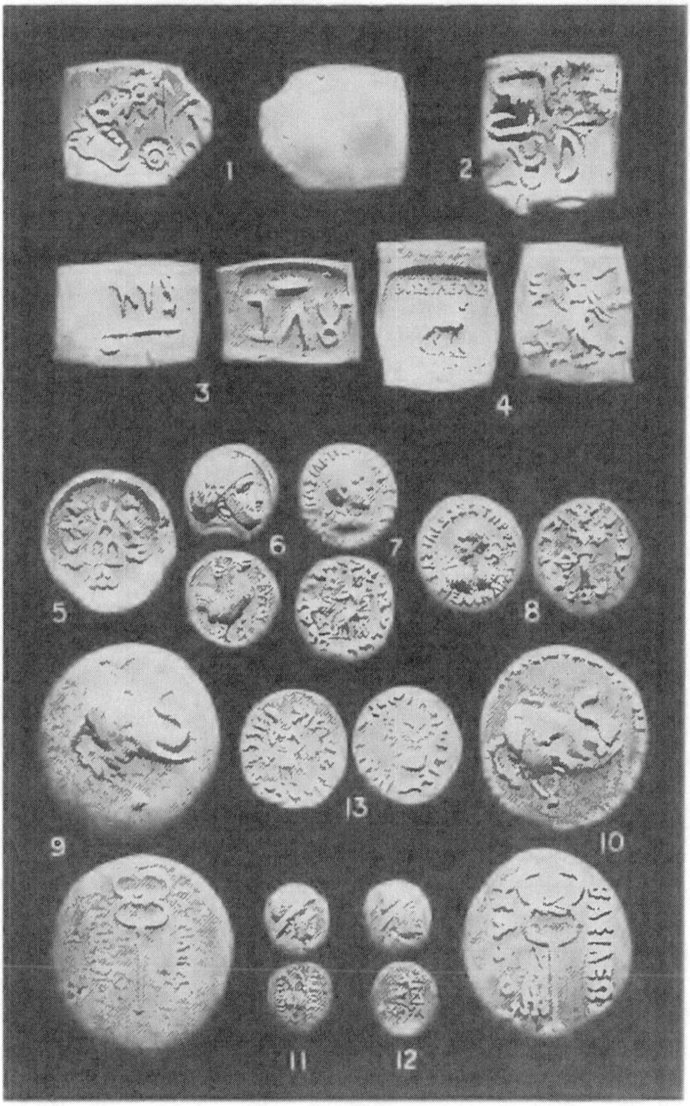

COINS OF ANCIENT INDIA. [See page 151.

titles of the king, and on the *reverse* a translation of this inscription in an Indian dialect and in Indian characters. As a first step in the process of decipherment, the names of the kings in their Indian guise were identified with the Greek. In this way a clue to the alphabet was obtained; and this clue soon led to the explanation of the Indian titles on the coins with their Greek equivalents; but it was only after many years of patient effort that the knowledge thus gained from the coin-legends was applied with complete success to the decipherment and translation of the long inscriptions, which are found in many parts of India, engraved on stone or copper plates.

These inscriptions, like the seals, are sometimes royal and sometimes private in character. The coin-legends are, naturally, royal. Both inscriptions and coins are often dated either in the year of some king's reign or in the year of some Indian era; and, if not actually dated, they are usually capable of being assigned, on archæological evidence, to some definite period and locality. They afford, therefore, positive information as to the history of royal houses in different parts of India. By their aid we may sometimes restore dynastic lists and determine the reigns of monarchs whose very names have otherwise vanished from the page of history.

But it was neither from Indian literature nor from inscriptions that there came the first ray of light to pierce the darkness in which the history of Ancient India lay enveloped. That light came from Greece.

For one short period only, and for one corner of India only, do we possess any connected narrative of events in the centuries before Christ. This is furnished by the Greek historians of the Indian campaigns of Alexander the Great in the years 327-5 B.C., and of his successor, Seleucus Nicator, in 305 B.C. These historians give some account of the rise to power of an Indian adventurer whom they call Sandrokottos. It was Sir William Jones who first recognised that Sandrokottos was to be identified with Chandragupta, who is known from Indian sources to have been the founder of the Maurya Empire, which at its height, in the reign of his grandson, Açoka, included, not only all the continent of India with the exception of the extreme South, but also the greater part of the countries now known as Afghānistān and Baluchistān. Within a few years of the departure of Alexander, the Greek dominions in North-Western India came under the sway of Chandragupta, and they were confirmed in his possession by the treaty of peace which he concluded with Seleucus in 305 B.C. It was certain, then, that the accession of Chandragupta to power in the Punjab must have taken place at some date between 325 and 305 B.C.

This identification of Sandrokottos with Chandragupta, which thus brought the Greek and Indian records into relation with each other, was long known as the 'sheet-anchor' of Indian chronology. It secured a fixed point from which it was possible to measure chronological distances with some approximation to certainty.

A number of other fixed points have since been gained, sometimes from one and sometimes from another of the three chief sources of Indian history —Indian literature, Indian inscriptions, and foreign authorities. Thus the period of the reign of Açoka, the third emperor of the Maurya dynasty, is determined by the mention in one of his inscriptions of five contemporary Hellenic sovereigns, whose dates are known from Greek history :—(1) Antiochus II. of Syria (B.C. 261-246); (2) Ptolemy Philadelphus of Egypt (B.C. 285-247); (3) Magas of Cyrene (B.C. 285-258); (4) Antigonus Gonatas of Macedon (B.C. 277-239); and (5) Alexander of Epirus (acc. B.C. 272).

The determination of the initial years of the various eras, in which the dates of inscriptions are commonly expressed, has further made it possible to arrange in systematic order the historical data which they supply. The Vikrama era of 58 B.C. and the Çaka era of 78 A.D. still continue to be used in different parts of India. The starting points of others have been determined by investigation, *e.g.*, the Traikūṭaka, Chedi, or Kalachuri era of 249 A.D. the Gupta era of 319 A.D., and the era of King Harshavardhana of 606 A.D. Each of these marks the establishment of a great power in some region of India, and originally denoted the regnal years of its founder.

A most important epoch in the religious history of India is marked by the rise of Jainism and Buddhism, the dates of which have been ascertained approximately from the combined evidence of literary and inscriptional sources. These two religions, which have much in common, represent the most successful of a number of movements directed against the formality of Brahmanism and the supremacy of the priestly caste in the sixth century B.C. The leaders of both were Kshatriyas or members of the princely and military caste. Vardhamāna Jñātaputra, the founder of Jainism, probably lived from 599 to 527 B.C., and Siddhārtha Gautama, the founder of Buddhism, from about 563 to 483 B.C.

These two reformed religions, although springing directly from Brahmanism and inheriting many of its fundamental ideas, yet introduce new elements into the intellectual life of India and are important factors in its subsequent civilization. For the period before their rise no positive dates are forthcoming. This earlier period is represented by a very large literature, which exhibits transformations of so far-reaching a character in the domain of language, of religion, and of social institutions, that centuries would seem to be required for their accomplishment. It is possible, by tracing the course of such changes, to distinguish different strata, as it were, in the literature, and so to establish a sort of relative chronology for this early period; but it is evident that all such dates as we may for the sake of convenience associate with this system of relative chronology must be conjectural. The ultimate limits within which this early period of Indian history must be confined are, on the one hand, suggested by the evidence of Comparative Philology and the spread of Indo-European civilization, and, on the other, fixed by the rise of Jainism and Buddhism.

CHAPTER II

THE CIVILIZATIONS OF INDIA

The names of India—Its natural limits—Its chief invaders—Dravidians—Aryans—Natural divisions of the continent—The geographical course of Aryan civilization.

THE word India originally meant the country of the river Indus. It is, in fact, etymologically identical with 'Sind.' In this restricted sense it occurs in the Avesta and in the inscriptions of King Darius (522-486 B.C.) as denoting those territories to the west of the Indus which, in the earlier periods of history, were more frequently Persian than Indian. It was this province which Alexander the Great claimed as conqueror of the Persian Empire. The name India became familiar to the West chiefly through Herodotus and the historians of Alexander's campaigns; and, in accordance with what would almost seem to be a law of geographical nomenclature, the name of the best known district was subsequently applied to the whole country.

In Sanskrit literature it is only at a comparatively

late period that we find any one word to denote the whole continent of India. This is intelligible, as all the early literature belongs to the Aryan civilization, the gradual extension of which from the north-west into the central region and eventually to the south may be traced historically; and the geographical outlook of this civilization would naturally be limited to the stage which it had reached at any particular time. A comprehensive term—*Bhārata* or *Bhārata-varsha*—seems to occur first in the epics. It means 'the realm of Bharata,' and refers to a legendary monarch who is supposed to have exercised universal sovereignty. The historical foundation for the name is found in the ancient Aryan tribe of the Bharatas, who are well known in the Rig-veda.

The limits of this continent of India or Bhārata-varsha, which is equal in extent to the whole of Europe without Russia, are for the most part well defined by nature. On the north, it is almost completely cut off from the rest of Asia by impassable mountain ranges; and it is surrounded by the sea on the eastern and western sides of the triangular peninsula which forms its southern portion. But the northern barrier is not absolutely secure. At its eastern and western extremities, river-valleys or mountain-passes provide means of communication with the Chinese Empire on the one hand and with Persia on the other. At the present time, these means of access to the Indian Empire have been practically closed in the interests of political security; but until the year 1738, when the Persian king Nādir Shāh invaded India and sacked Delhi, the very capital of its Mughal emperors, countless hordes of Asiatic tribes have swarmed down the valleys or over the passes which lead into India. Hence the extraordinary diversity of races and languages which, now united under one sway for the first time in history, together constitute the Indian Empire. A glance at the ethnographical and linguistic maps of India will show that the races and languages on the east are Mongolian, and those on the west Persian or Scythian in character; while the Aryan civilization which predominates in the north is the result of invasions which can be traced historically, and the Dravidian civilization which still holds its own in the south is probably also due to invasions in prehistoric times.

The chief motive of the migration of peoples, which forms one of the most important factors in the history of the human race, was scarcity of food; and the chief cause of this scarcity has in Central Asia been the gradual desiccation of the land. However this desiccation may have arisen, whether through physical causes which affect the whole of our planet, or through the thrusting up, by shrinkage of the earth's crust, of lofty mountain-ranges which cut off the rain-bearing winds from certain regions, or again by man's improvidence in the destruction of forests and the neglect of natural means of irrigation, it is a phenomenon the progress of which may be traced to some extent historically. Explorations in Baluchistān and Seistān have brought to light the monuments of past civilizations which perished because of the drying up of the land; and above all the researches of Sir Aurel Stein in Chinese Turkestān have supplied us with materials and observations from which it will be possible eventually to write the history of desiccation in this part of the world with some chronological precision. Archæological evidence proves that this region which is now a rainless desert, in which no living being can exist because of the burning heat and blinding sand-storms in summer and the arctic cold in winter, was once the seat of a flourishing civilization; and the study of the written documents and works of art, discovered at the various ancient sites which have been explored, shows that these sites were abandoned one by one at dates varying from about the first century B.C. to the ninth century A.D. The import ance of these observations, as bearing on the history of India, lies in the consideration that its present isolation on the land-side was by no means so complete in former times, when the river-valleys and mountain-passes on the east and west of the Himālayas were open, and when the great high-roads leading from China to India on the east, and from India through Baluchistān or Afghānistān to Persia and so to Europe on the west, not only afforded a constant means of communication, but also permitted the migration of vast multitudes.

The invaders from the east, greatly as they have modified the ethnology and the languages of India, have left no enduring record whether in the advancement of civilization or in literature. Invaders from the west, on the other hand, have determined the character of the whole continent. In our sketch of the civilization of Ancient India, we shall have to deal especially with two of these invasions—the Dravidian and the Aryan.

It has sometimes been supposed that the Dravidians were the aborigines of India; but it seems more probable that these are rather to be sought among the numerous primitive tribes, which still inhabit mountainous districts and other regions difficult of access. Such, for example, are the Gonds, found in many different parts of India, who remain even to the present day in the stone age of culture, using flint implements, hunting with bows and arrows, and holding the most rudimentary forms of religious belief. The view that the Dravidians were invaders, who came into India from the north-west in prehistoric times, receives support from the fact that the Brāhūī language, spoken in certain districts of Baluchistān, belongs to the same family as the Dravidian languages of Southern India; and it is possible that it may testify to an ancient settlement of the Dravidians before they invaded India. In any case, Dravidian civilization was predominant in India before the coming of the Aryans. Many of the Dravidian peoples now speak Aryan or other languages not originally their own; but they still retain their own languages and their characteristic social customs in the South, and in certain hilly tracts of Central India; and there can be no doubt that they have very greatly influenced Aryan civilization and Aryan religion in the North. Their literatures do not begin until some centuries after the Christian era, but the existence of the great Dravidian kingdoms in the South may be traced in Sanskrit literature and in inscriptions from a much earlier period.

The term Aryan was formerly, chiefly through the influence of the writings of Max Müller, used in a broad sense so as to include the whole family of Indo-European languages. It is now almost universally restricted to the Persian and Indian groups of this family, as being the distinctive title used in their ancient scriptures.

These two groups have in common so many characteristic features, in regard to which they differ from the other members of the family, that we can only conclude that there must have been a period in which the ancestors of the Persians of the Avesta and of the Indians of the Rig-veda lived together as one people and spoke a common language. When a separation took place, the Persian Aryans occupied Bactria, the region of Balkh, *i.e.*, Afghānistān north of the Hindu Kush, and Persia, while the Indian Aryans crossed over the passes of the Hindu Kush into the valley of the Kābul River in southern Afghānistān, and thence into the country of the Indus, *i.e.* the North-Western Frontier Province and the northern Punjab. The date of this separation cannot be determined with much accuracy. The most ancient literatures of the two peoples—the Indian Rig-veda, possibly as early as 1200 B.C., and the Persian Avesta, dating from the time of Zoroaster, probably about 660-583 B.C.—afford no conclusive evidence from which it is possible to estimate the distance of time which separates them from the period of unity; but an examination of the two languages seems to indicate that the common speech from which they are derived did not differ materially from that of the Rig-veda, since Avestan forms are, from the etymological point of view, manifestly later than Vedic forms, and may generally be deduced from them by the application of certain well ascertained laws of phonetic change. It may be inferred, then, that the Aryan migration into India took place during a period which is separated by no long interval from the date of the earliest Indian literature.

The progress of Aryan civilization in India is determined naturally by the geographical conformation of the continent, which is divided into three well-defined principal regions:—

(1) North-Western India, the country of the Indus and its tributaries. This region, bounded by mountainous districts on the north and west, is separated from the country of the Ganges and Jumna on the east by the deserts of Rājputāna. With it has often been associated in history the country of Gujarāt (including Cutch and Kāthiāwār) to the south.

(2) Hindustān, the country of the Ganges and the Jumna and their tributaries, the great plain which constitutes the main portion of Northern India.

(3) The Deccan or 'Southern' (Skt. *dakshiṇa*) India, the large triangular table-land lying south

of the Vindhya Mountains, together with the narrow strips of plain-land which form its fringe on the eastern and western sides.

The first of these regions is in character transitional between India and Central Asia. Into it have poured untold waves of invasion—Persian, Greek, Scythic, Hun, etc.—and many of these have spent their force within its limits. Hence its extraordinary diversity in race, language, and religion. The second has been the seat of great kingdoms, some of which, both in the Hindu and in the Muhammadan periods, have grown by conquest into mighty empires including the whole of Northern India and considerable portions, but never the whole, of the South. It has always included most of the chief centres of religious and intellectual life in India. The third region has a character of its own. The history of its kingdoms and their struggle for supremacy among themselves have usually been enacted within its own borders. It has, as a rule, successfully resisted the political, and has only by slow degrees admitted the intellectual, influence of the North; but when it has accepted ideas or institutions it has held them with great tenacity, so that the South is now in many respects the most orthodox and the most conservative portion of the continent.

The literary and inscriptional records of Ancient

India enable us to trace with a remarkable degree of continuity the course of Aryan civilization through the periods during which it passed from the first of these regions into the second and then eventually into the third. But it must always be remembered that these records are partial, in the sense that they represent only one type of civilization and only those countries to which this civilization had extended at any particular epoch. Unless this fact be borne constantly in mind, the records are apt to produce the impression of a unity and a homogeneity in the political, religious, and social life which never existed. The best corrective for this false impression is to study Ancient India always in the light of our knowledge of Modern India and in the light of general history. India is and, in historical times, always has been composed of a number of large countries and a multitude of smaller communities, each having its own complicated racial history and each pursuing its own particular lines of development independently of its neighbours. In India, as in Europe, one or other of the constituent countries has from time to time succeeded in creating a great empire at the expense of its neighbours. But the mightiest of these empires, that of the Maurya kings of Magadha in the third century B.C., and that of the Mughal kings of Delhi at its height in the last years of the seventeenth century A.D., have never been co-extensive with the continent; they have never included the extreme south of India. They were won by conquest and maintained by power; and, when the power failed, the various countries which constituted these empires reasserted their independence. Such a phenomenon as the British dominion in India, which is founded less on conquest than on mutual advantage—which holds together some 773,000 square miles of British territory (excluding Baluchistān and Burma) and nearly the same amount (745,000 square miles) of independent territory administered by about 650 native princes and chiefs, principally because the great common interest of all alike is peace and security—finds no parallel in history. Neither has religion at any time formed a complete bond of union between these multitudinous and diverse nationalities. The Brahmanical systems of thought and practice founded on the Vedas have never gained universal acceptance, as some of their text-books might lead us to suppose. Not only was their supremacy contested even in the region which was their stronghold—the country of the Ganges and the Jumna—by reformed religions such as Jainism and Buddhism; but their appeal was everywhere almost exclusively to the higher castes who can never have formed the majority of the population. Most of the people, no doubt, in Ancient as in Modern India, were either confessedly, or at heart and in practice, followers of more primitive forms of faith. As Mr W. Crooke says, in describing present religious conditions (*Imperial Gazetteer of India*, i. p. 432), "The fundamental religion of the majority of the people—Hindu, Buddhist, or even Musalmān—is mainly animistic. The peasant may nominally worship the greater gods; but when trouble comes in the shape of disease, drought, or famine, it is from the older gods that he seeks relief."

CHAPTER III

THE PERIOD OF THE VEDAS

The Rig-veda — Oral transmission — Geography — State of Civilization— Religion—Germs of the later caste-system—The Sāma-veda—The Yajur-veda—Contrasted with the Rig-veda—The Atharva-veda—The principal divisions of Northern India in Vedic times.

THE Sanskrit word *veda* comes from the root *vid* 'to know,' which occurs in the Latin *vid-eo* and in the Anglo-Saxon *wit-an*, from which our English forms *wit*, *wisdom*, etc. are derived. It is especially used to denote the four collections of sacred 'wisdom,' which form the ultimate basis on which rest not only all the chief systems of Indian religion and philosophy, but also practically the whole of the Aryan intellectual civilization in India, whether sacred or secular. The most ancient of these collections is the Rig-veda, or 'the Veda of the Hymns.' It consists of 1028 hymns intended to accompany the sacrifices offered to the various deities of the ancient Indian pantheon. In respect of style and historical character it may be compared most fittingly to the

'Psalms of David' in the Hebrew scriptures. If compared by the number of verses, it is rather more than four times as long.

Internal evidence, supplied by changes in language and progress in thought, shows that the composition of the hymns of the Rig-veda must have extended over a considerable period. They were handed down from generation to generation in the families of the 'rishis,' or sacred bards, who composed them; and, at a later date, when their venerable antiquity had invested them with the character of inspired scriptures, they were collected together and arranged on a two-fold plan, firstly, according to their traditional authorship, and secondly, according to the divinities to whom the hymns in each group were addressed. Like all the other works of the Vedic period the Rig-veda has been transmitted orally from one generation to another from a remote antiquity even down to the present day. If all the manuscripts and all the printed copies were destroyed, its text could even now be recovered from the mouths of living men, with absolute fidelity as to the form and accent of every single word. Such a tradition has only been possible through the wonderfully perfect organization of a system of schools of Vedic study, in which untold generations of students have spent their lives from boyhood to old age in learning the sacred texts and in teaching them to their pupils. This is, beyond all question, the most marvellous instance of unbroken continuity to be found in the history of mankind; and the marvel increases when we consider that this extraordinary feat of the human memory has been concerned rather with the minutely accurate preservation of the forms of words than with the transmission of their meaning. The Brahmans, who, for long centuries past, have repeated Vedic texts in their daily prayers and in their religious services, have attached little or no importance to their sense; but so faithfully has the verbal tradition been maintained by the Vedic schools that 'various readings' can scarcely be said to exist in the text of the Rig-veda which has come down to us. It has probably suffered no material change since about the year 700 B.C., the approximate date of the *pada-pāṭha* or 'word-text,' an ingenious contrivance, by which each word in the sentence is registered separately and independently of its context, so as to supply a means of checking the readings of the *saṃhitā-pāṭha* or 'continuous text,' and thus preventing textual corruption. But the sense of many Vedic words was either hopelessly lost or extremely doubtful nearly two thousand five hundred years ago, when Yāska wrote his *Nirukta*. In fact, at that period the

Vedic language was already regarded as divine; and its obscurities in no way tended to detract from its sacred character—for, as the commentator, Sāyaṇa (died 1387 A.D.), quoting a popular maxim of the time, says: "It is no fault of the post if the blind man cannot see it"—but rather to strengthen the belief in its super-human origin. Orthodox Hindus, then as now, believed that the Vedas were the revealed word of God, and so beyond the scope of human criticism. It remained, therefore, for Western scholars in the nineteenth century, who were able to approach the subject without prepossessions, not only to bring to light again the original meaning of many passages of the Rig-veda, but also to show the historical significance of the whole collection as one of the most interesting and valuable records of antiquity.

The region in which the hymns of the Rig-veda were composed is clearly determined by their geographical references. About twenty-five rivers are mentioned; and nearly all of these belong to the system of the Indus. They include not only its five great branches on the east, from which the Punjab, 'the land of the five rivers,' derives its name, but also tributaries on the north-west. We know, therefore, that the Aryans of the Rig-veda inhabited a territory which included portions of S.E. Afghānistān, the N.-W. Frontier Province, and the Punjab.

Like many later invaders of India, they, no doubt, came into this region over the passes of the Hindu Kush range of mountains. Sanskrit literature subsequent to the date of the Rig-veda enables us to trace the progress of their Aryan civilization in a south-easterly direction until the time when it was firmly established in the plains of the Jumna and the Ganges. These two great rivers were known even in the times of the Rig-veda; but at that period they merely formed the extreme limit of the geographical outlook.

The type of civilization depicted in the Rig-veda is by no means primitive. It is that of a somewhat advanced military aristocracy ruling in the midst of a subject people of far inferior culture. There is a wide gulf fixed between the fair-skinned Aryans and the dark Dasyus—the name itself is contemptuous, meaning usually 'demons'—whom they are conquering and enslaving. This distinction of colour marks the first step in the development of the caste-system, which afterwards attained to a degree of rigidity and complexity unparalleled elsewhere in the history of the world.

The conquerors themselves are called comprehensively 'the five peoples'; and these peoples are divided into a number of tribes, some of whom are to be traced in later Indian history. The Aryan tribes were not always united against the people of the land, but sometimes made war among themselves. Each tribe was governed by a king; and the kingly office was usually hereditary, but sometimes, perhaps, elective. As among other Indo-European peoples, the constitution of the tribe was modelled on that of the family; and the king, as head, ruled with the aid and advice of a council of elders who represented its various branches. Thus, the state of society was patriarchal: but it was no longer nomadic. The people lived in villages, and their chief occupations were pastoral and agricultural.

In war, the chief weapons were bows and arrows, though swords, spears, and battle-axes were also used. The army consisted of foot-soldiers and charioteers. The former were probably marshalled village by village and tribe by tribe as in ancient Greece and Germany, and as in Afghānistān at the present day. The war-chariots, which may have been used only by the nobles, carried two men, a driver and a fighting man who stood on his left.

In the arts of peace considerable progress had been made. The skill of the weaver, the carpenter, and the smith furnish many a simile in the hymns.

The metals chiefly worked were gold and copper. It is doubtful if silver and iron were known in the age of the Rig-veda.

Among the favourite amusements were hunting, chariot-races, and games of dice—the last mentioned a sad snare both in Vedic times and in subsequent periods of Indian history.

The religion of the Aryan invaders of India, like that of other ancient peoples of the same Indo-European family—Greeks, Romans, Germans, and Slavs—was a form of nature worship, in which the powers of the heavens, the firmament, and the earth were deified. Thus Indra, the god of the storm, is a giant who with his thunderbolt shatters the stronghold of the demon and recovers the stolen cows, even as the lightning-flash pierces the cloud and brings back the rains to earth; while Agni (the Latin *ignis*), the god of fire, is manifested in heaven as the sun, in the firmament as the lightning, and on earth as the sacrificial fire produced mysteriously from the friction of the fire-sticks. The sacrifice is the link which connects man with the gods, who take delight in the oblations, and, in return, shower blessings —wealth in cows and horses, and strength in the form of stalwart sons—on the pious worshipper. There are also other aspects of this religion. The spirits of the departed dwell in 'the world of the

Fathers,' where they are dependent for their sustenance on the offerings of their descendants; and ever lurking around man are the demons of famine and disease, whose insidious attacks can only be averted through the favour of the beneficent deities.

A certain amount of this Vedic mythology is common to other Indo-European peoples, as is proved by such equations as the following:—

Skt. *Dyaús pitár-*, 'the Sky-father'=Gk. *Zeús patḗr*=Lat. *Jū-piter*=Anglo-Saxon *Tīw* (cf. *Tīwes dæg*=Eng. *Tuesday*).

Skt. *Ushā́sa-*, 'the Dawn'=Gk. *Eṓs* for * *Āusōs*=Lat. *Aurōra* for * *Ausōsa* = Anglo-Saxon *ēas-t* (Eng. *east*).

Points of similarity with the ancient Persian religion are more numerous; and, in estimating their cogency as evidence that the Persian and Indian Aryans dwelt together for some period after their separation from the other branches of the Indo-European stock, we must bear in mind the fact that the Persian religion, as represented in the Avesta, is the outcome of the reforms of Zoroaster (660-583, B.C.) which, presumably, did away with much of its ancient mythology. It must suffice here to mention one striking feature which the two religions share in common. The Vedic offerings of *soma*, the intoxicating juice of a plant, find their exact counterpart in the Avestan *haoma*, a word which is etymologically identical.

The hymns of the Rig-veda were the work of priestly bards who took no small pride in their poetic skill; and, although we may find much monotony in the collection, due to the great number of hymns which are sometimes devoted to the same topic, and numerous difficulties and obscurities, caused chiefly by our own defective knowledge of the language and of the period, yet the beauty and strength of many of the hymns are such as fully to justify this pride. The principles of scansion are determined by the number of syllables in each line, by a *cæsura* after the fourth or fifth syllable, and by quantity, as in Greek and Latin, except that the rigid scheme of short and long is generally confined to the endings of the lines. The commonest metres are of eight, eleven, or twelve syllables to the line, and three or four of these lines usually make a verse. But there are a number of other varieties, some of them more complicated in structure.

The office of priest, therefore, required not only a knowledge of the ritual of the sacrifice, but also some skill in the making of hymns. No doubt, originally the king of the tribe was supreme in sacred as in secular matters; and it is possible that certain indications of this earlier state of affairs may still survive in the Rig-veda. But already, by a natural division of labour, the performance of the ordinary sacrifices on the king's behalf was in practice entrusted to a priest specially appointed, who was called *purohita* (=Latin, '*præfectus*'). This office, too, had probably become hereditary, and it tended to grow in importance with the strengthening of the religious tradition.

Thus, although in the early period of the Rig-veda, the caste-system was unknown—the four castes are only definitely mentioned in one of the latest hymns—yet the social conditions which led to its development were already present. As we have seen, the first great division between conquerors and conquered was founded on colour. In fact, the same Sanskrit word, *varṇa*, means both 'colour' and 'caste.' This was the basis on which a broad distinction was subsequently drawn between the 'twice-born,' *i.e.* those who were regularly admitted into the religious community by the investiture of the sacred cord, and the servile caste or Çūdras. The three-fold divisions of the 'twice-born' into the ruling class (Kshatriyas), the priests (Brāhmaṇas), and the tillers of the soil (Vaiçyas) finds its parallel in other Indo-European communities, and indeed it seems to represent the natural distribution of functions which occurs generally in human societies at a similar stage of advancement.

Of the more primitive inhabitants of the land the Rig-veda teaches us little, except that they were a pastoral people possessing large herds of cattle and having as defences numerous strong holds. Contemptuous references describe them as a dark-complexioned, flat-faced, 'noseless' race, who spoke a language which was unintelligible, and followed religious practices which were abhorrent to their conquerors. Of all the rest of India beyond the country of the Rig-veda we know nothing whatever at this period.

Of the three other Vedas two are directly dependent on the Rig-veda. They are especially intended for the use of the two orders of priests who took part in the sacrifices in addition to the Hotar who recited the verses selected from the Rig-veda. The Sāma-veda, which chiefly consists of verses from the Rig-veda 'pointed' for the benefit of the Udgātar or singing priest, has little or no historical value. The Yajur-veda, which contains the sacrificial formulæ to be spoken in an undertone by the Adhvaryu, while he performed the manual portions of the ceremony, is on the other hand a most important document for the history of the period to which it belongs. It introduces us not only to a new region, but also to a complete transformation of religious and social conditions.

The Yajur-veda marks a further advance in the trend of Aryan civilization from the country of the North-West into the great central plain of India. Its geography is that of Kuru-kshetra, 'the field of the Kurus,' or the eastern portion of the plain which lies between the Sutlej and the Jumna, and Pañchāla, the country to the south-east between the Jumna and the Ganges. This region, bounded on the west by the sacred region which lay between the rivers Sarasvatī (Sarsūti) and Dṛishadvatī (Chautang), was the land in which the complicated system of Brahmanical sacrifices was evolved, and it was in later times regarded with especial reverence as 'the country of the holy sages,' while the first home of the Aryan invaders of India seems to have been almost forgotten. Kuru-kshetra is also the scene of the great battle which forms the main subject of the national epic, the Mahābhārata. One of its capitals was Indraprastha, the later Delhi, which became the capital of the whole of India under the Mughal emperors, and which has recently, in 1912, been restored to its former proud position.

Religious and social conditions, as reflected in the Yajur-veda, differ very widely from those of the period of the Rig-veda. All the moral elements in religion seem to have disappeared, extinguished by an elaborate and complicated system of ceremonial which is regarded no longer as a means of worship but as an end in itself. Sin in the Rig-veda means the transgression of the divine laws which govern the universe: in the Yajur-veda it means the omission—whether intentional or accidental—of some detail in the endless succession of religious observances which filled man's life from birth to death. The sacrifice had developed into a system of magic by means of which supernatural powers might be attained; and the powers thus gained might be used for any purpose, good or bad, spiritual or temporal, and even to coerce the gods themselves. In the Yajur-veda also, the earlier stages of the caste-system, in essentially the form which it bears to the present day, are distinctly seen. Not only are the four great social divisions hardening into castes, but a number of mixed castes also are mentioned. Thus were fixed the outlines of the system which subsequently, by further differentiation according to trades, etc., became extraordinarily complicated. The tremendous spiritual power, which the sacrifice placed in the hands of the priestly caste, was no doubt the cause which directly led to the predominance of this caste in the social system.

The religion and the social system of the Yajur-

NOTES ON THE ILLUSTRATIONS

THE GIRNAR ROCK IN 1869

(Plate I, Frontispiece, and Plate V A, facing p. 150)

GIRNĀR, the Sanskrit *Girinagara*, the 'Hill City,' was in ancient times the name of Junāgadh in Kāthiāwār. It is now applied to the sacred mountain on the east of the city. At the foot of this mountain stands a rock which is without question one of the most interesting and valuable of all historical monuments. It is about twelve feet in height and seventy-five feet in circumference at the base; and it has engraved on its surface records of three kings belonging to three different dynasties which have ruled over Western India:—(1) Açoka, the Maurya Emperor, *c.* 250 B.C.; (2) Rudradāman, the Mahākshatrapa or 'Great Satrap' of Surāshṭra and Mālava (inscription dated in the year 72 of what was called at a later date the Çaka era = 150 A.D.); and (3) Skandagupta, the Gupta Emperor (inscription bearing dates in the years 136, 137, and 138 of the Gupta era beginning in 319 A.D. = 455, 456, and 457 A.D.).

The illustration is from a photograph taken by Dr James Burgess in 1869. Since that date the rock has been protected from further injury by a roof. The fourteen edicts of Açoka are engraved on the north-east face of the rock and cover a space of about 100 square feet. The inscription of Rudradāman occupies the top, and the inscription of Skandagupta the west face.

The edicts of Açoka have already been described (*v.* pp. 105-8). The subjoined reproduction of an impression of the second edict will serve to illustrate the beautiful Brāhmī writing of the period—the letters in the original are about two inches

Atharva-veda is not sufficient to enable us to determine the precise locality in which it was compiled; but the tribes mentioned in it indicate that the full extent of the two first regions occupied by the Aryan civilization during the earlier and later Vedic periods—the country or the Indus and the country of the Ganges and the Jumna—was known at the time when the collection was made.

For a long period, Aryan civilization was confined within these limits. The definitions of the whole region, and of its chief divisions, are thus given in *The Laws of Manu*, a work, in its present form, of a much later date, but undoubtedly representing the traditions from Vedic times:—

Āryāvarta, 'the country of the Aryans,' is the district lying between the Himālaya and the Vindhya Mountains, and extending from the eastern to the western sea.

Madhya-deça, 'the Middle Country,' is that portion of *Āryāvarta*, which lies between the same two mountain ranges, and is bounded by *Vinaçana* (the place where the river Sarasvatī loses itself in the sand) on the west, and by *Prayāga* (the modern Allahābād, where the Ganges and the Jumna meet) on the east.

Brahmarshi-deça, 'the country of the holy sages,' includes the territories of the Kurus, Matsyas,

Pañchālas and Çūrasenas (*i.e.* the eastern half of the State of Patiāla and of the Delhi division of the Punjab, the Alwar State and adjacent territory in Rājputāna, the region which lies between the Ganges and the Jumna, and the Muttra District in the United Provinces).

Brahmāvarta, 'the Holy Land,' lies between the sacred rivers Sarasvatī (Sarsūti) and Dṛishadvatī (Chautang), and may be identified generally with the modern Sirhind. Its precise situation is somewhat uncertain, owing to the difficulty of tracing the courses of rivers in this region; for many of them lose themselves in the sand and sometimes reappear at a distance of several miles. That Brahmāvarta formed part of Kuru-kshetra is seen from the following verse from the Mahābhārata:—

"*Dakshiṇena Sarasvatyā Dṛishadvatyuttareṇa cha*
Ye vasanti Kurukshetre, te vasanti Trivishṭape."

"Those, who dwell in Kuru-kshetra to the south of the Sarasvatī and the north of the Dṛishadvatī, dwell in Heaven."

CHAPTER IV

THE PERIOD OF THE BRĀHMAṆAS AND UPANISHADS

Growth of a prose literature—Contents of the Brāhmaṇas—Language—Geography—The Çatapatha Brāhmaṇa—Its relation to Buddhism and to the ancient Sanskrit epics—The religion of works and the religion of knowledge—The Upanishads—Pantheism—The intellectual movement not confined to the priestly caste.

THE most ancient works of Indian literature, with which we have been dealing hitherto, are almost entirely in verse. This fact is in accordance with the general rule that poetry precedes prose in the development of literature. The only prose to be found in the Vedas occurs in some versions of the Yajur-veda, where a sort of commentary is associated with the verse portions. From this point of departure, we may trace the growth of a large prose literature of a similar character. Each of the Vedas was handed down traditionally in a number of priestly schools devoted entirely to its study, and each of these schools produced in the course of time its own particular text-book, in the form of an elaborate prose treatise, intended to explain to the priest the mystical significance of that portion of the sacrificial ceremony which he was called upon to perform. These treatises are styled Brāhmaṇas or 'religious manuals.' Their contents are of the most miscellaneous character; but they may be classified broadly under three categories:—(1) directions (*vidhi*), (2) explanations (*arthavāda*), and (3) theosophical speculations (*upanishad*). The last were, as we shall see, developed more fully in a special class of works bearing the same title. The Brāhmaṇas presuppose an intimate acquaintance with the very complicated ritual of the sacrifice; and they would have been unintelligible to us, if we had not fortunately also possessed the later 'Sūtras,' in which each separate branch of Vedic lore is minutely explained.

The Brāhmaṇas are priestly documents in the narrowest and most exclusive sense of the term. At first sight, their contents would seem to be the most hopeless possible form of historical material. It is only incidentally and accidentally that they afford any insight whatever into the political and social conditions of the country and the period to which they belong. They give an utterly one-sided view even of the religion. But religion had other and nobler aspects even in this priest-ridden age, and the memorial of these is preserved in the Upanishads.

Nevertheless, there are found embedded in the Brāhmaṇas a number of old-world legends which supply valuable evidence for the history of primitive human culture. For instance, a reminiscence of the far distant period, in which human sacrifices prevailed, is to be seen in a story told in the Aitareya Brāhmaṇa (VII. iii.) of the Rig-veda, about a Brahman lad named Çunaḥçepa, who was about to be sacrificed to the god Varuṇa, when the god himself appeared and released him. Another story in the same Brāhmaṇa (II. i.) illustrates the stages of transition from human sacrifice, in which at first some animal, and subsequently a cake made of rice, was in ordinary practice substituted for the human victim.

Occasionally also some valuable information as to the social and political state of India may be gleaned from the Brāhmaṇas. The coronation ceremonies referred to in the eighth book of the Aitareya Brāhmaṇa show how completely the priestly caste had, in theory at least, gained supremacy over the kingly caste. The same book, moreover, shows an extension of the geographical horizon, for it mentions by name a number of the peoples of Southern India. It also records the kingly titles used in different regions of India;

and these titles seem to show that, at this early period, the most diverse forms of government ranging from absolute monarchies to self-governing (*svarāj*) communities were to be found. This interpretation would certainly be in accordance with what we know from the inscriptions and other historical sources of a later date. The interesting fact, that the Brahmanical religion did not include all the tribes of Aryan descent, is gathered from the account given in the Tāṇḍya Brāhmaṇa of certain sacrifices (the *vrātya-stomas*), which were performed on the admission of such Aryans into the Brahman community. The description of these non-Brahmanical Aryans—"they pursue neither agriculture nor commerce; their laws are in a constant state of confusion; they speak the same language as those who have received Brahmanical consecration, but nevertheless call what is easily spoken hard to pronounce" (trans. in Weber, *Ind. Lit.*, p. 67)—shows that they were freebooters speaking the Prakrits or dialects allied to Sanskrit.

For the student of language the Brāhmaṇas possess the highest interest. They are perfect mines of philological specimens. They show a great variety of forms which are transitional between the language of the Rig-veda and the later Classical Sanskrit; and as being, together with the prose portions of the Yajur-veda, the oldest examples of Indo-European prose, they afford materials for the study of the development from its very first beginnings of a prose style and of a more complicated syntax than is feasible in ordinary verse. Thus we find, existing side by side in India at the same period, an ancient poetry, no longer primitive in character but elaborated by many generations of bards, and a rudimentary prose, which often reminds us of the first attempts of a child or an uneducated person to express his thoughts in writing.

The geography of the Brāhmaṇas is generally the land of the Kurus and Pañchālas, 'the country of the holy sages'; but at times it lies more to the west or more to the east of this region. The Çatapatha Brāhmaṇa is especially remarkable for its wide geographical outlook. Some of its books belong to the first home of the Aryan invaders in the north-west. In others the scene changes from the court of Janamejaya, king of the Kurus, to the court of Janaka, king of Videha (Tirhut or N. Bihār). The legend of Māṭhava, king of Videgha (the older form of Videha), in the first book, indicates the progress of Brahmanical culture from the 'Holy Land' of the Sarasvatī, first into Kosala (Oudh), and then over the river Sadānīra (probably the Great Gandak, a tributary of the Ganges) which formed its boundary, into Videha.

The Çatapatha Brāhmaṇa supplies an important link in the history of religion and literature in India; for it is closely connected with Buddhism on the one hand, and with the ancient Sanskrit epics on the other. Many of the terms which subsequently became characteristic of Buddhism, such as *arhat* 'saint' and *çramaṇa* 'ascetic,' first occur in the Çatapatha; and among the famous teachers mentioned in it are the Gautamas, the Brahman family whose patronymic was adopted by the Kshatriya family in which Buddha was born. It was to Janamejaya, king of the Kurus, that the story of one of the great epic poems—the Mahābhārata—is said to have been related; while Janaka, king of Videha, is probably to be identified with Janaka, the father of Sītā, the heroine of the other great epic, the Rāmāyaṇa.

Such are some of the comparatively few features of general interest which relieve the dreary monotony of the endless ritualistic and liturgical disquisitions of the Brāhmaṇas. As we have seen, the kind of religion depicted in the Brāhmaṇas is absolutely mechanical and unintelligent. The hymns from the Rig-veda are no longer used with any regard to their sense, but verses are taken away from their context and strung together fantastically, because they all contain some magical word, or because the scheme of their metres, when arranged according to the increasing or decreasing number of syllables, resembles a thunderbolt wherewith the sacrificer may slay his foes, or for some other equally valid reason. Such a system may have been useful enough to secure the supremacy of the Brahmans and to keep the common people in their proper place; but it is not to be imagined that it can ever have satisfied the intellectual aspirations of the Brahmans themselves; and, as a matter of fact, there has always been in India a broad distinction between a 'religion of works,' intended for the common people and for the earlier stages in the religious life, and a 'religion of knowledge' which appealed only to an intellectual aristocracy. Certain hymns of reflection in the Rig-veda and the Atharva-veda show that the eternal problems of the existence and the nature of a higher power, and of its relation to the universe and to man, were already filling the thoughts of sages even at this early period; and, as we have seen, theosophical speculation finds its place even in the Brāhmaṇas. It is, however, specially developed in certain treatises, called Upanishads, which usually come at the end of the Brāhmaṇas, separated from them by Āraṇyakas or 'forest-books,' which are transitional in character as in position. Thus the whole of Vedic literature, which is comprehensively styled *çruti* or 'revelation' as distinguished from the later *smṛiti* or 'tradition,' falls into two great classes. The Vedas and Brāhmaṇas belong to the 'religion of works,' and the Āraṇyakas and Upanishads to the 'religion of knowledge.'

A similar principle of division applies also to the four *āçramas*, or religious stages, into which the life of the Brahman is theoretically divided. In the first, he lives as a pupil in the family of his *guru* and learns from him the sacred texts and the sacrificial procedure; in the second, he marries and brings up a family, religiously observing all the domestic rites; in the third, after he has seen the face of his grandson, he goes forth into the forest, either accompanied by his wife or alone, to live the life of an anchorite; and in the fourth, he abandons all earthly ties and devotes himself to meditation on the *ātman* or 'Supreme Soul.' In this way, his life is divided between the 'religion of works' in the two first, and the 'religion of knowledge' in the two last stages.

The Upanishads, with which the philosophical hymns of the Rig-veda and the Atharva-veda are closely connected in spirit, lead us into the realm of what we should call philosophy rather than religion. But the two have never been separated in India, where the latter has always been regarded as the necessary preparation for the former. Orthodoxy consists in the unquestioning acceptance of the social system and the religious observances of Brahmanism. Beyond this, speculation is free to range without restriction, whether it lead to pantheism, to dualism, or even to atheism.

The Upanishads are not systematic. They contain no orderly expositions of metaphysical doctrine. They give no reasons for the views which they put forth. They are the work of thinkers who were poets rather than philosophers. But nevertheless they contain all the main ideas which formed the germs of the later systems of philosophy, and are, therefore, of the utmost importance for the history of Indian thought.

The object of the 'religion of knowledge' is neither earthly happiness nor the rewards of heaven. Such may be the fruits of the 'religion of works.' But, according to Indian ideas, the joys of earth and of heaven are alike transient. They may be pursued by the man of the world who mistakes appearances for realities; but the sage turns away from them, for he knows that, as the result of works, the human soul is fast bound in a chain of mundane existences, and that it will go on from birth to birth, whether in this world or in other worlds, its condition in each state of existence being determined by the good or evil deeds performed in previous existences. His sole aim, therefore, is to obtain *mukti*, or 'release,' from this perpetual succession of birth and re-birth. This release can only be obtained by 'right knowledge,' that is to say, by the full realization of the fact that there is no existence, in the highest and only true sense of the term, except the *ātman* or the 'World-Soul.' In reality everything is the ātman and the ātman is everything. There is no second 'being.' All that seems to us to exist besides the ātman is 'appearance' or 'illusion.' It is some disguise of the ātman, due merely to a change in name and form. Just as all the vessels which are made of clay, by whatever names they may be called and however many different forms they may assume, are in reality only clay, so everything, which appears to us to have an independent existence, is really only a modification of the ātman. There is, therefore, no essential difference between the soul of the individual and the 'World Soul.' The complete apprehension of this fact constitutes the 'right knowledge,' which brings with it 'release' from the circle of mundane existences, which are now clearly seen to be apparent only and not real.

This pantheistic doctrine, which forms the main, but by no means the exclusive, subject of the Upanishads, was, at a later period, developed with marvellous fulness and subtilty in the Vedānta system of philosophy. Its influence has been more potent than any other in moulding the spiritual and intellectual life of India even down to the present day.

The evidence of language shows that the earliest Upanishads, which are also the most important, belong to the period of the later Brāhmaṇas. Regarded as sources for the history of religion and civilization in India, these two classes of words supplement and correct each other. The Brāhmaṇas represent the ceremonial, and the Upanishads the intellectual, phase of religion; and the social aspects of these two phases stand in striking contrast. While the performance of the sacrifice, with all its complicated ritual, remained entirely in the hands of the priestly caste, members of the royal caste and even learned ladies joined eagerly in the discussions, which were held at royal courts, concerning the nature of the ātman, and acquitted themselves with distinction. Thus the far-famed Brahman, Gārgya Bālāki, came to Ajātaçatru, the king of Kāçī (Benares), and, having heard his words of wisdom, humbly begged that he might be permitted to become his pupil; while the ladies Gārgī and Maitreyī discoursed concerning these deep matters, on perfectly equal terms, with Yājñavalkya, the great rishi of the court of Janaka, king of Videha. The time of the Upanishads was, in fact, one of great spiritual unrest, and of revolt against the formalism and exclusiveness of the Brahmanical system. In this revolt the royal caste played no unimportant part; and, as we shall see in the next chapter, the leaders of the two chief religious reforms, known as Jainism and Buddhism, were both scions of princely families.

CHAPTER V

THE RISE OF JAINISM AND BUDDHISM

The founders of Jainism and Buddhism—Their doctrines contrasted with Brahmanism—Their literatures—The Sanskrit epics—The Purāṇas—Genealogies—The Pali epics—The Sūtras.

WITH the rise of Jainism and Buddhism we enter the period of Indian history for which dates, at least approximately correct, are available. We are no longer dependent for our chronology on an estimate of the length of time required for the evolution of successive phases of thought or language.

These two religions differ from the earlier Brahmanism in so far as they repudiate the 'religion of works' as inculcated in the Vedas and the Brāhmaṇas. That is to say, they deny the authority of the Vedas and of the whole system of sacrifice and ceremonial which was founded on the Vedas; and in so doing they place themselves outside the pale of Brahman orthodoxy. On the other hand, their fundamental ideas are substantially those of the 'religion of knowledge' as represented in the Upanishads. These ideas are, in fact, the postulates on which all Indian religions and all Indian philosophies rest. They hold, one and all, that the individual soul is fast bound by the power of its own *karma* or 'actions' to a continuous series of birth and re-birth which need never end; and the object of one and all is to find out the way by which the soul may be freed from the bonds of this unending mundane existence. They differ from one another, partly in regard to the means whereby this freedom may be obtained, and partly in their views as to the nature of the universe and of the individual soul, and as to the existence or non-existence of some being or some first cause corresponding to the *Ātman* or 'World-Soul' of the Upanishads.

Vardhamāna Jñātaputra, the founder of Jainism, called by his followers *Jina* (hence the epithet 'Jain') 'the Conqueror' or *Mahāvīra* 'the Great Hero,' probably lived from about 599 to 527 B.C. As his surname denotes, he was a scion of the Kshatriya or princely tribe of Jñātas, and he was related to the royal family of Vaiçālī (Basārh) in Videha (Tirhut). His system of teaching, as it has come down to us, is full of metaphysical subtilties; but, apart from these, its main purpose, summed up in a few words, is to free the soul from its mundane fetters by means of the 'three jewels'—a term also used in Buddhism, but in a different sense—viz. 'right faith,' 'right knowledge,' and 'right action,' each of these headings being divided and subdivided into a number of dogmas or rules of life.

The Jains still form a wealthy and important section of the community in many of the large towns, particularly in Western India, where their ancestors have left behind them an abiding record in the beautiful temples of Gujarāt. They have also played a notable part in the civilization of Southern India, where the early literary development of the Kanarese and Tamil languages was due, in a great measure, to the labours of Jain monks.

The founder of Buddhism—the *Buddha* or 'Enlightened' as he was called by his disciples—was Siddhārtha, whose date was probably from about 563 to 483 B.C. He belonged to the Kshatriya tribe of Çākyas, and so is often styled 'Çākya-muni,' the sage of the Çākyas; but, in accordance with a practice which prevailed among the Kshatriyas, he bore a Brahman surname, Gautama, borrowed from one of the ancient families of Vedic Rishis. The Çākyas ruled over a district in what is now known as the Western Tarai of Nepāl; and, at Buddha's period, they were feudatories of the king of Kosala (Oudh). In recent years some most interesting archæological discoveries have been made in this region, perhaps the most interesting of all being the inscribed pillar which was erected, *c.* 244 B.C., by the Buddhist emperor Açoka to mark the spot where the Buddha was born.

Buddha shared the pessimism of his period, the literature of which constantly reminds us of the words of the Preacher—'Vanity of vanities: all is vanity'—and he sought a refuge from the world and a means of escape from existence, first in the doctrine of the Ātman, as set forth in the Upanishads, and subsequently in a system of the severest penance and self-mortification. But neither of these could satisfy him; and after a period of meditation he propounded his own system, which in its simplest form is comprised in the four headings of his first sermon at Benares:—"sorrow: the cause of sorrow: the removal of sorrow: the way leading to the removal of sorrow." That is to say, all existence is sorrow; this sorrow is caused by the craving of the individual for existence, which leads from birth to re-birth; this sorrow can be removed by the removal of its cause; this removal may be effected by following the eight-fold path, viz. 'right understanding,' 'right resolve,' 'right speech,' 'right action,' 'right living,' 'right effort,' 'right mindfulness,' 'right meditation.' It will be seen, then, that the 'eight-fold path' of Buddhism is essentially identical with the 'three jewels' of the Jains, and that both of them differ from the Upanishads chiefly in substituting a practical rule of life for an abstract 'right knowledge,' as the means whereby 'freedom' may be secured.

Jainism and Buddhism also differ materially from Brahmanism in their organization. Brahmanism is strictly confined to the caste-system, in which a man's social and religious duties are determined once and for all by his birth. Jainism and Buddhism made a wider claim to universality. In theory, all distinction of castes ceased within the religious community. In practice, the firmly established social system has proved too strong for both religions. It is observed by the Jains at the present day, while, in India itself, it has re-absorbed the Buddhists many centuries ago. Brahmanism is not congregational. Its observances consist partly of caste-duties performed by the individual, and partly of sacrifices and ceremonies performed for his special benefit by priests. In ancient times there were, therefore, no Brahman temples. Jainism and Buddhism were, on the contrary, both congregational and monastic. One striking result of this difference is that the most ancient monuments of India teach us a great deal about the Jains and Buddhists and little or nothing about the Brahmans. The one-sided impression, which the comparative lack of this important species of evidence for the earliest history of Brahmanism is apt to produce, must be corrected from a study of the literature.

The language of Brahmanism is always and everywhere Sanskrit. The language of the Jain and Buddhist scriptures is that of the particular district or the particular period to which the different books or versions belong.

Buddhism disappeared entirely from India proper at the end of the twelfth century A.D., but it still flourishes at the northern and southern extremities, in Nepāl and Ceylon. From its original home it has extended far and wide into Eastern Asia; and its ancient books are preserved in four great collections:—Pali (in Ceylon, Burma, and Siam), Sanskrit (in Nepāl), Tibetan, and Chinese.

Thus both Jainism and Buddhism arose and flourished originally in the same region of India, viz. the districts to the east of the 'Middle Country,' including the ancient kingdoms of Kosala, Videha, and Magadha, *i.e.* the modern Oudh together with the old provinces of Tirhut and S. Bihār in Western Bengal. They spread subsequently to other regions, and for many centuries divided the allegiance of India with Brahmanism.

Both religions produced large and varied literatures, sacred and secular, which are especially valuable from the historical point of view, as they represent traditions which are, presumably, independent of one another and of Brahmanism. We may, therefore, reasonably believe in the accuracy of a statement if it is supported by all the three available literary sources, Brahman, Jain, and Buddhist, since it is almost certain that no borrowing has taken place between them. The chief difficulty which the historian finds in using these materials lies in the fact that the books in their present form are not original. They are the versions of a later age; and it is not easy to determine to what extent their purport has been changed by subsequent additions or corrections, or by textual corruption.

This remark is especially true of some of the Brahman sources. For instance, the ancient epic poems, the Mahābhārata and the Rāmāyaṇa, and the Purāṇas or 'old-world stories' are undoubtedly, in their present form, many centuries later than the date of some of the events which they profess to record, and their evidence, therefore, must be used with caution. But it can scarcely be questioned that much of their substance is extremely ancient, although the form in which it is expressed may have undergone considerable change in the course of ages.

The Mahābhārata, or 'great poem of the descendants of Bharata,' consists of about 100,000 couplets usually of thirty-two syllables each. That is to say, if reckoned by the number of syllables, it is about thirty times as long as Milton's 'Paradise Lost.' Only about a fifth of this mass has anything whatever to do with the main story, viz. the war between the Kurus and the Pāṇḍus. All the rest is made up of episodes, or disconnected stories, or philosophical poems. There can be no doubt that the Mahābhārata, as it stands now, is the creation of centuries; and criticism has succeeded in distinguishing various stages in its growth and in assigning certain probable limits of date to these stages. It must suffice here to say that the historical groundwork of the story would seem to be an actual war at a remote period between the well-known Kurus and the Pāṇḍus, whose history is obscure; and that an epic poem, which forms the nucleus of the present Mahābhārata, was put together at least as early as the fourth century B.C. from traditional war songs founded on events which took place at a much earlier date.

While the Mahābhārata belonged originally to the 'Middle Country,' the Rāmāyaṇa belongs rather to the districts lying to the east of this region. As its title denotes, it celebrates 'the story of Rāma,' a prince of the royal Ikshvāku family of Kosala (Oudh), and its heroine is his faithful wife Sītā, daughter of Janaka, king of Videha (Tirhut). Unlike the Mahābhārata, the Rāmāyaṇa is, on the whole, probably the product not only of one age but also of one author, Vālmīki. It is not entirely free from more recent additions; but the main poem forms one consistent whole, and such indications of date as can be found seem to show that it was composed probably in the fourth or third century B.C. As we have seen, some of its characters appear to be far more ancient and to be mentioned in the Upanishads.

There can be no doubt that, originally at least, the ancient epics belonged rather to the Kshatriyas than to the Brahmans. Their scenes are courts and camps, and their chief topics the deeds of kings and warriors. Their religion is that of the kingly caste. Among their deities, Indra, who was especially the sovereign lord of the kings of the earth, stands most prominent, and the future reward which awaits their heroes for the faithful discharge of kingly duty is a life of material happiness in Indra's heaven. Their language is neither that of the Brāhmaṇas and Upanishads, nor that which is known as Classical Sanskrit. It is less regular and more popular in character than either of these; and like all poetical languages it preserves many archaisms. We can scarcely be wrong in supposing that this epic Sanskrit was formed by the minstrels who wandered from court to court singing of wars and heroes. At a later date, when the supremacy of the Brahman caste was firmly established, no doubt a more definitely religious tone was given to the epics. The history of the Mahābhārata, in fact, seems to show such a transition from a purely epic to a didactic character. Originally the story of a war, such as would appeal chiefly to the military caste, it has become through the accretions of ages—the work, no doubt, of Brahman editors—a vast encyclopædia of Brahmanical lore.

Closely connected in character with the Mahābhārata are the Purāṇas. The word *purāṇa* means 'ancient'; and the title is justified by the nature of the contents of the eighteen long Sanskrit poems which are so called. These consist chiefly of legendary accounts of the origin of the world and stories about the deeds of gods, sages, and monarchs in olden times. Works of this description and bearing the same title are mentioned in the Atharva-veda and in the Brāhmaṇas. This species of literature must, therefore, be extremely old, and there can be no doubt that much of the subject-matter of the early Purāṇas has been transmitted to the later versions. But, in their present form, the Purāṇas are undoubtedly late, since some of the dynasties which they mention are known to have ruled in the first six centuries of the Christian era. Together with these, however, they mention others which belong to the last six centuries B.C., and others again which they attribute to a far more remote antiquity. It is evident that the Purāṇas have been 'brought up to date' and wilfully altered so frequently, that their ancient and modern elements are now often inextricably confused.

In theory, these 'family genealogies' (*vaṃçā-nucharita*) constitute one of the five essential features of a Purāṇa: they are supposed to form part of the prophetic description given by some divine or semi-divine personage, in a far remote past, of the ages of the world to come and of the kings who are to appear on earth. They are, therefore, invariably delivered in the future tense. Such lists are absent from many of the modern versions, but, where they do occur, there can be no doubt that they were originally historical. Occasionally they give not only the names of the kings, but also the number of years in each reign and in each dynasty. The information which they supply is supported, to some extent, by the literatures of the Jains and

Buddhists, and, to some extent, by the evidence of inscriptions and coins. But, in the course of time, these lists have become so corrupt, partly through textual errors, and partly through the 'corrections' and additions of editors, that, as they stand at present, they are neither in agreement with one another nor consistent in themselves. Nevertheless, the source of many of their errors is easily discovered; and it is quite possible that, when these errors have been removed from the text by critical editing, many of the apparent discrepancies and contradictions of the Purāṇas may likewise disappear.

A somewhat similar problem is presented also by the Pali epic poems of Ceylon. The Dīpavaṃsa in its present form dates from the fourth century A.D. and the Mahāvaṃsa from the sixth century A.D.; but both are almost certainly founded on traditional chronicles which were far more ancient. The professed object of both is to record the history of Buddhism from the earliest times, and in particular its history in the island of Ceylon from the date of its introduction by Mahendra (Mahinda) *c.* 246 B.C. to the reign of Mahāsena, at the beginning of the fourth century A.D. There can be little doubt that, when the miraculous elements and other later accretions are removed from these chronicles, there remains a substratum of what may fairly be regarded as history.

The period to which the earliest Jain and Buddhist literature belongs is marked by the growth of a species of composition—the Sūtra—which is peculiarly Indian. It is used by all sects alike and applied to every conceivable subject, sacred or secular. The Sūtras may, perhaps, most aptly be said to represent the codification of knowledge. The word means 'thread'; and a treatise bearing the title consists of a string of aphorisms forming a sort of analysis of some particular subject. In this way all the different branches of learning—sacrificial ritual, philosophy, law, the study of language, etc.—which were treated somewhat indiscriminately in earlier works such as Brāhmaṇas and Upanishads were systematized. The Sūtra form was, no doubt, the result of a method of instruction which was purely oral. The teacher, as we know from the extant Buddhist Sūtras, was wont to enunciate each step in the argument and then to enforce it by means of parallel illustrations and by frequent reiteration until he had fully impressed it on the pupil's mind. The pupil thus learned his subject as a series of propositions, and these he remembered by the aid of short sentences which became in the course of time more and more purely mnemonic. The Sūtras are therefore, as a rule, unintelligible by themselves and can only be understood with the help of a commentary. They preserve a wonderfully complete record both of the social and religious life and of intellectual activity in almost every conceivable direction, but they are unhistorical in character and rarely throw any light, even incidentally, on the political conditions of the times and countries to which they belong.

All the literary sources, Brahman, Jain, and Buddhist, are in general agreement as to the chief political divisions of Northern India in the sixth and fifth centuries, B.C. The number of large kingdoms mentioned in the lists is usually sixteen; but in addition to these there were many smaller principalities, and many independent or semi-dependent communities, some of which were oligarchical in their constitution. The chief feature in the subsequent history is the growth of one of the large kingdoms, Magadha (S. Bihār), which was already becoming predominant among the nations east of the Middle Country during Buddha's lifetime. It eventually established an empire which included nearly the whole of the continent of India.

CHAPTER VI

THE INDIAN DOMINIONS OF THE PERSIAN AND MACEDONIAN EMPIRES

Relations between India and the West—Kings of Mitanni—Cyrus—Inscriptions of Darius—Herodotus—Ctesias—Gandhāra and 'India'—Expedition of Xerxes against Greece—Alexander the Great—Arrian—Q. Curtius Rufus—Alexander's Indian campaigns—Limits of his conquests—His Indian satrapies—India after his death.

WE have seen that the present political isolation of India is a comparatively modern feature in its history, and that, in ancient times, many of the physical impediments also, which now prevent free communication both with the Farther East and with the West, did not exist. We have seen that the results of such communication in prehistoric times are attested by the certain evidence of ethnology and language. We now approach the period during which relations between India and the West (Western Asia and Europe) are to be traced in historical records.

The region of Western Asia, which lies between India and the Ægean and Mediterranean Seas,

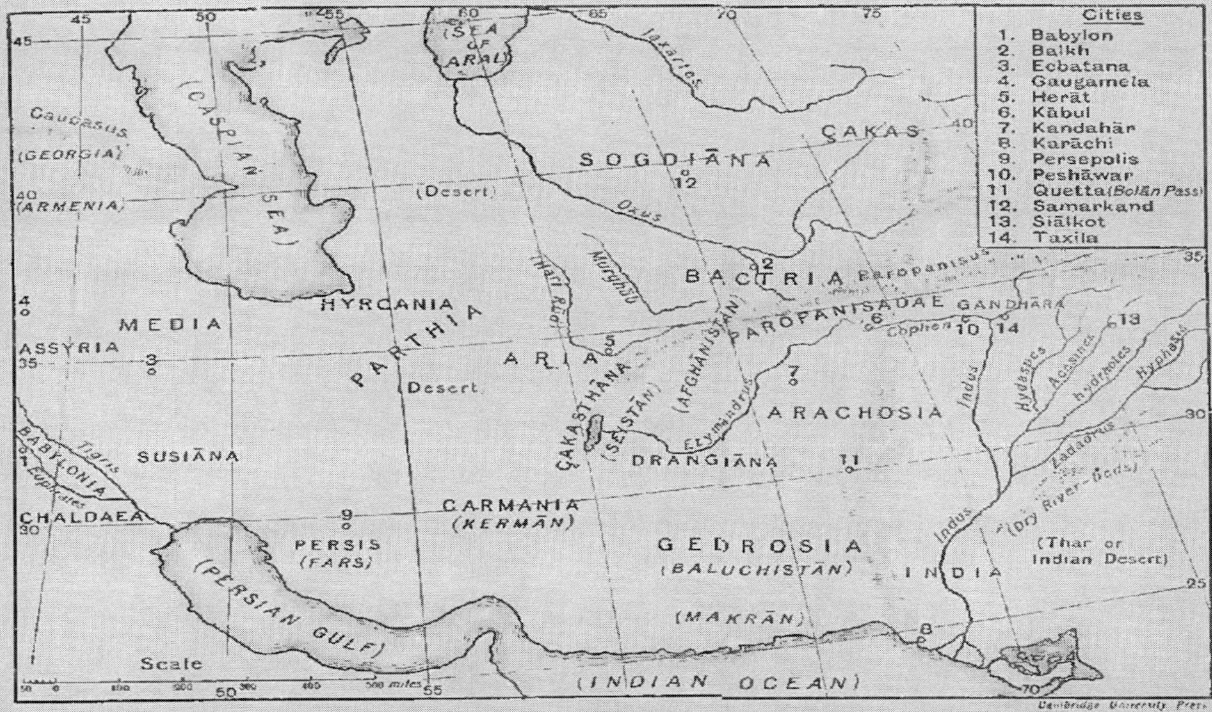

MAP OF N.W. INDIA AND ADJACENT COUNTRIES IN THE TIME OF ALEXANDER THE GREAT.

that is to say the region which comprises the modern countries of Afghānistān, Baluchistān, Persia, and the northern provinces of Turkey in Asia (Armenia, Asia Minor, Mesopotamia, and Syria) is famous as the site of many of the most advanced civilizations of antiquity. In extent, it is larger than the continent of India, but less than India and Burma combined. Here, as in India, many peoples of different races and languages have played their part on the stage of history; and here, too, now one and now another of these peoples has, from time to time, become predominant among its fellows and has succeeded in establishing a great empire. As in the case of India also, the history of these ancient civilizations has been recovered from the past by modern scholarship. Excavations of ancient sites in the valleys of the Tigris and Euphrates, and elsewhere in this region, have brought to light thousands of inscriptions in cuneiform characters, not one syllable of which could have been read a hundred years ago. These inscriptions, now that many of them have been deciphered, tell of Assyrian and Babylonian civilizations which were flourishing at least as early as 2200 B.C., and of a still earlier Sumerian civilization, the monuments of which seem to go back to about 4000 B.C.

Of especial interest from the point of view of

Indian history are the cuneiform inscriptions which relate to the kings of Mitanni, a branch of the Hittites established in the district of Malatia in Asia Minor; for we learn from them that not only did the kings of Mitanni in the fifteenth and fourteenth centuries B.C. bear Aryan names, but also that they worshipped the deities of the Rig-veda—Indra, Varuṇa, Mitra, and the Açvins (the horsemen gods, the Castor and Pollux of Indian mythology), under their Vedic title 'Nāsatyā.' The precise manner in which the kings of Mitanni and the Aryans of the Rig-veda were connected must remain for the present uncertain; but, as many ancient sites in this region are still unexplored and as only a portion of the inscriptions already discovered have yet been published, there seems to be no limit to the possibilities presented by this most fertile field of archæology, and it is not improbable that both this and many other obscure problems may still be solved.

That there may have been constant means of communication both by land and sea between the Babylonian Empire and India seems extremely probable; but, although there are traditions, there is no real evidence that the sway of any of the powers of Western Asia extended to the east as far as India, until the time of Cyrus (558-530 B.C.), the founder of the Persian Empire, to whom, on the authority of certain Greek and Latin authors, is attributed the conquest of Gandhāra. This geographical term usually denotes the region comprising the modern districts of Peshāwar in the N.-W. Frontier Province and Rāwalpindi in the Punjab, but in the Old Persian inscriptions it seems to include also the district of Kābul in Afghānistān. This province formed the eastern limit of a vast empire which, in the reign of Cyrus, included not only the whole of Western Asia as described above, but other countries to the north of India and Afghānistān, and in the reign of his successor Cambyses (530-522 B.C.) also Egypt.

Gandhāra thus forms a most important link connecting India with the West; and it holds a unique position among all the countries of India from the fact that its history may be traced with remarkable continuity from the times of the Rig-veda even down to the present day. Its inhabitants, the Gandhāris, are mentioned both in the Rig-veda and the Atharva-veda; and Gandhāra appears among the countries of India in Sanskrit literature from the period of the Upanishads onwards, in the earliest Buddhist literature, and in the most ancient Indian inscriptions. It remained a Persian province for about two centuries; and, after the downfall of the empire in 331 B.C., it, together with the Persian province of 'India' or 'the country of the Indus,' which had been added to the empire by Darius not long after 516 B.C., came under the sway of Alexander the Great. Through Gandhāra and the Indian province was exercised the Persian influence, which so greatly modified the civilization of North-Western India.

The sources, from which our knowledge of the Indian dominions of the Persian Empire is derived, are of two kinds:—(1) the inscriptions of King Darius I (522-486 B.C.), and (2) Greek writers, notably Herodotus and Ctesias.

The historical inscriptions of Darius are at three important centres in the ancient kingdom of Persia—Behistun, Persepolis, and Naksh-i-Rustam. They are engraved in cuneiform characters and in three languages—Old Persian, Susian, and Babylonian. The Behistun inscription, cut into the surface of a lofty cliff at a height of about 500 feet above the ground, is famous in the annals of scholarship; for it was through the publication of its Old Persian version by Sir Henry Rawlinson in 1847, that the numerous difficulties in the decipherment of the cuneiform alphabet were finally overcome. The historical importance of these inscriptions lies in the fact that they contain lists of all the subject peoples, and therefore indicate the extent of the Persian Empire at the time when they were engraved.

The chief object of the 'Histories' of Herodotus is to give an account of the struggles between the Greeks and the Persians during the period from 501 to 478 B.C. His third book contains a list of the twenty 'nomes' or fiscal units, into which Darius divided the empire, together with the names of the peoples included in each and the amount of tribute imposed. Herodotus both confirms and amplifies the information supplied by the inscriptions. His work is by far the most valuable record of the Persian Empire which has come down to us.

Ctesias resided at the Persian court for seventeen years (*c.* 415-398 B.C.) as physician during the reigns of Darius II (424-404 B.C.), and Artaxerxes Mnemon (404-358 B.C.). He wrote accounts both of Persia and India of which there are extant fragments preserved by later writers, as well as abridgements made by Photius, patriarch of Constantinople, in the ninth century A.D. The writings of Ctesias relating to India are, in the form in which they have survived, descriptive of the races and the natural productions of the country rather than historical.

Such information as may be gleaned from the available sources as to the political history of the Persian provinces of Gandhāra and 'India' may thus be summarized.

Gandhāra is said to have been conquered during the reign of Cyrus. The writers to whom we owe this information certainly lived several centuries after the time of Cyrus, but it is not improbable that they may have possessed good authority for their statements. In the Behistun inscription of Darius, the date of which is about 516 B.C., the Gandharians appear among the subject peoples in the Old Persian version; but their place is taken in the Susian and Babylonian versions by the Paruparaesanna. These were the inhabitants of the Paropanisus, or Hindu Kush. As a rule, a distinction may be observed between the country of the Paropanisadae (the Kābul Valley, in Afghānistān) and Gandhāra, but the two names seem to be used indiscriminately in these inscriptions, probably as denoting generally the region which included both. In the inscriptions at Behistun no mention is made of the 'Indians' who are included with the Gandharians in the lists of subject peoples given by the inscriptions on the palace of Darius at Persepolis and on his tomb at Naksh-i-Rustam. From this fact it may be inferred that the 'Indians' were conquered at some date between 516 B.C. and the end of the reign of Darius in 486 B.C. The preliminaries to this conquest are described by Herodotus, who relates that Scylax was first sent by Darius (probably about 510 B.C.) to conduct a fleet of ships from one of the great tributaries of the Indus in the Gandhāra country to the sea, and to report on the tribes living on both banks of the river.

Although it is not possible to determine the precise extent of the 'Indian' province thus added by Darius to the Persian Empire, yet the information supplied by Herodotus indicates with sufficient clearness that it must have included territories on both sides of the Indus from Gandhāra to its mouth, and that it was separated from the rest of India on the east by vast deserts of sand, evidently the present Thar or Indian Desert. The 'Indian' province, therefore, no doubt included the Western Punjab generally and the whole of Sind. According to Herodotus it constituted the twentieth and the most populous fiscal division of the empire and it paid the highest annual tribute of all. The Gandharians are placed together with three other peoples in the seventh division, which paid altogether less than half that amount.

During the reigns of Darius and his successor Xerxes took place the Persian expeditions against Greece, the total defeat of which by a few small states forms one of the most stirring episodes in history. The immediate cause of the war between Persians and Greeks was the revolt, in

501 B.C., of the Greek colonies in Ionia, the district along the western coast of Asia Minor, which had become tributary to Persia after the defeat of Crœsus, king of Lydia, by Cyrus in 546 B.C. The Ionians were aided by the Athenians, who thus incurred the hostility of the Persians; and, after the revolt was subdued, the Persian arms were turned against Greece itself.

Since the Persians thus became acquainted with the Greeks chiefly through the Ionian colonists, they not unnaturally came to use the term *Yaunā* 'Ionians,' which occurs in the inscriptions of Darius, in a wider sense to denote Greeks or people of Greek origin generally. The corresponding Indian forms (Skt. *Yavana* and Prakrit *Yona*), which were borrowed from Persia, have the same meaning in the Indian literature and inscriptions of the last three centuries before and the first two centuries after the Christian era. At a later date, these terms were used in India to denote foreigners generally.

Of the most powerful of the Persian expeditions against Greece, which was accompanied by King Xerxes in person in 480 B.C., Herodotus has preserved a full account. It was made up of contingents sent by no fewer than forty-nine subject nations of the Persian Empire, and it is said to have numbered more than two million six hundred thousand fighting men. In this vast army both of the Persian provinces of India were represented, the Gandharians being described by Herodotus as bearing bows of reed and short spears, and the 'Indians' as being clad in cotton garments and bearing similar bows with arrows tipped with iron.

After the time of Herodotus, the history of Northern India, as told by Greek writers, almost ceases until the period when both Greece and Persia had submitted to the Macedonian conqueror, Alexander the Great. But it is important to remember that this lack of information is to a great extent accidental and due to the fact that the writings of Ctesias have only survived in fragments, and that other writings have been lost. There is no reason to doubt that the Indian provinces were included in the Persian Empire and continued to be governed by its satraps until the end. There is also no reason to doubt that during the whole of this period the Persian Empire formed a link which connected India with Greece. We know that the battles of the Persian king were fought, to a very great extent, with the aid of Greek mercenaries, and that Greek officials of all kinds readily found employment both at the imperial court and at the courts of the satraps. At no period in early history, probably, were the means of communication by land more open, or the conditions more favourable for the interchange of ideas between India and the West.

But the event which, in the popular imagination, has, for more than twenty-two centuries past, connected India with Europe, is undoubtedly the Indian expedition of Alexander the Great. He came to the throne of Macedon in 336 B.C., at the age of twenty; and, after subduing Greece, he crossed over the Hellespont and began the conquest of Western Asia in 334 B.C. After the defeat of the Persian monarch, Darius III Codomannus, at the decisive battle of Gaugamela in 331 B.C., the Persian dominions in India together with all the rest of the empire came nominally under the sway of the conquerors. The military campaigns which followed had, as their ostensible object, the vindication of the right of conquest and the consolidation of the empire thus won.

The route by which Alexander approached India passed through the Persian provinces of Aria (Herāt in North-Western Afghānistān), Drangiāna (Seistān, in Persia, bordering on South-Western Afghānistān), and Arachosia (Kandahār in South-Eastern Afghānistān), and thence into the country of the Paropanisadae (the Kābul Valley, the province of East Afghānistān which adjoins the present North-Western Frontier Province). Here, in the spring of 329 B.C., he founded the city of Alexandria-sub-Caucasum, 'Caucasus' being the name which the Greeks gave to the Paropanisus (Hindu Kush), the great chain of mountains which in ancient times separated India from Bactria, and which now divides Southern from Northern Afghānistān. This city Alexander used as his base of operations; and hence he made a series of campaigns with the object of subduing the Persian provinces which lay to the north—Bactria (Balkh) and Sogdiāna (Bukhāra). On his return to the city which he had founded, he began to make preparations for the invasion of India in the summer of 327 B.C.

If we reckon from this time to the actual date of Alexander's departure from India in the autumn of 325 B.C., the total duration of the campaign in India, that is to say the Kābul Valley, the North-Western Frontier Province, the Punjab, and Sind, was about two years and three months. As has been observed, this period is unique in the history of Ancient India in so far as it is the only one of which detailed accounts have come down to us.

The names are recorded of about twenty Greek writers, who are known to have composed histories of this campaign. Some of them actually accompanied Alexander, while the others were his contemporaries. But all their works without exception have perished. We, however, possess five different accounts of Alexander and his exploits by later authors to whom these original records were accessible. Of these the two most important are Arrian and Curtius.

Arrian, who was born about 90 A.D. and died in the reign of the Roman Emperor, Marcus Aurelius (161-180 A.D.), wrote in Greek an account of Alexander's Asiatic expedition, called the 'Anabasis of Alexander,' which was modelled on the 'Anabasis' of Xenophon, and also a book on India, which was founded on the work of Megasthenes and intended to supplement the account of Ctesias. Arrian is our most trustworthy authority.

Q. Curtius Rufus, whose date is somewhat doubtful, wrote a work on the exploits of Alexander which has, with some probability, been assigned to the reign of Claudius (41-54 A.D.). This historical biography has been more praised for its literary merits than for its accuracy.

The difficulties, which the reader encounters in his endeavours to trace the progress of Alexander's campaign in India with the aid of these and other classical authorities, are very considerable. In the early stages of the campaign, the military operations of Alexander and his generals were carried out in the mountainous districts of Afghānistān and the North-Western

Frontier Province which lie between Kābul and the Indus. This region, then as now, was inhabited by numerous warlike tribes living in a perpetual state of feud with one another. Even to the present day much of its geography is scarcely known to the outer world. The fights with warlike tribes and the sieges of remote mountain strongholds, which the historians of Alexander describe in detail, find their parallels in the accounts of the military expeditions, which the Indian government is obliged to send from time to time to quell disturbances on the North-Western Frontier. Even now it is scarcely possible to follow the course of such expeditions, as described in books or newspapers, without the aid of special military sketch-maps drawn to a large scale. The difficulty is greatly increased when our only guides are ancient records, in which the identification of place-names with their modern representatives is often uncertain. Thus, to cite perhaps the most striking instance of this uncertainty, no episode in Alexander's career has been more famous through the ages than his capture of the rock Aornos, a stronghold which was fabled to have defied all the efforts of Hercules himself, and no subject has attracted more attention on the part of students of Indian history than the identification of its present site;

but, in spite of all the learning and ingenuity which have been brought to bear on the point during the last seventy years, the geographical position of Aornos still remains to be decided.

Early in the spring of 326 B.C., Alexander and his army passed over the Indus, probably by means of a bridge of boats at Ohind, about sixteen miles above Attock, into the territories of the king of Taxila, who had already tendered his submission. Taxila (Sanskrit *Takshaçilā*), the capital of a province of Gandhāra, was famous in the time of Buddha as the great university town of India, and is now represented by miles of ruins in the neighbourhood of Shāhdheri in the Rāwalpindi District. From this city Alexander sent a summons to the neighbouring king, Porus, calling upon him to surrender. The name, or rather title, 'Porus,' probably represents the Sanskrit *Paurava*, and means 'the prince of the Pūrus,' a tribe who appear in the Rig-veda. Porus, who ruled over a kingdom situated between the Hydaspes (Jhelum) and the Acesines (Chenāb), returned a defiant answer to the summons, and prepared to oppose the invaders at the former river with all his forces. The ensuing battle, in which the Macedonian forces finally prevailed, is the most celebrated in the history of Alexander's Indian campaign. His conquests were subsequently extended, first to the

Hydraotes (Rāvi), and then to the Hyphasis (Beās), which marks their limit in an easterly direction. His soldiers refused to go farther, in spite of the eagerness of their leader.

Beyond the Beās dwelt the people whom the Greek historians call 'Prasioi.' This name is, no doubt, intended to represent the Sanskrit *Prāchyāḥ*, 'the Easterns,' and is a collective term denoting the nations of the country of the Ganges and Jumna. The Greek and Latin writers speak of them as of one great nation; but, as we have seen, this region included a number of large king doms and a multitude of smaller states. It is, however, quite possible that, at this period, all these kingdoms and states were united under the suzerainty of Magadha. Hitherto Alexander had not been brought face to face with any great confederation of the nations of India. He had conquered some states and accepted the allegiance of others; but none of these could, in all probability, be compared in point of strength with any of the great nations of Hindustān. It is useless to speculate as to what might have been the result if Alexander had crossed the Beās and come into conflict with the combined forces of the Prasioi.

After the refusal of the army to proceed, Alexander retraced his line of march to the

Hydaspes (Jhelum), on either bank of which he had previously founded a city—Bucephala, in honour of his favourite charger, Bucephalus, probably near the modern town of Jhelum, on the right bank, at the point where his army had crossed the river, and Nicaea, 'the city of victory,' on the left bank, on the site of the battle with Porus. At these cities Alexander collected the fleet which was to convey a large portion of his forces down the rivers of the Punjab to the mouth of the Indus, and thence through the Arabian Sea to the head of the Persian Gulf.

But Alexander's career of conquest in India was not finished. He had hitherto not only reclaimed the Persian province of Gandhāra, but had annexed the whole of the Northern Punjab which lay beyond, as far as the River Beās. He now proceeded, on his return journey, to reclaim the Persian province of 'India,' viz. the Western Punjab and Sind.

The command of the fleet was entrusted to Nearchus, who thus performed for Alexander a somewhat similar task to that which, nearly two centuries before, had been undertaken by Scylax at the command of Darius. Nearchus wrote an account of his adventures which is no longer extant, but which is quoted frequently by Arrian in his *Anabasis of Alexander*. The progress of the fleet as, protected by armies marching on either bank, it passed down the Jhelum into the Chenāb, and so into the Indus, is described by the Greek and Latin historians with their usual minuteness. The ordinary difficulties, which the reader finds in tracing the course of their narrative on the map of India, are here increased by the fact that all the rivers of the Punjab are known to have changed their courses. Such changes have been very considerable during the few centuries for which accurate observations are available, and the rivers must, accordingly, in many cases, have flowed in very different channels at the time of Alexander, more than two thousand two hundred years ago. We are, therefore, now deprived, to a great extent, of the chief means by which it is often possible to identify the modern position of ancient historical sites. But, although it may not always be easy to follow the details of the constant series of military operations which marked the journey to the sea, the final result of these operations is certain. The conqueror of the Persian Empire had fully established his claim to be the suzerain of the peoples who were formerly included in its 'Indian' province.

Before leaving India in the autumn of 325 B.C., Alexander had made provision for the future control of his new dominions by the appointment of satraps to govern the different provinces. In so doing he was merely perpetuating the system which had become firmly rooted in Northern India as the result of two centuries of Persian rule. The satraps whom he selected as governors in the former provinces of the Persian empire were Greek or Persian; while, in the case of the newly added territories, he seems, where possible, to have chosen the native prince as satrap. Alexander, in fact, carried into practice the traditional Indian policy recommended by Manu (vii. 202), and followed, wherever it has been possible or expedient, by conquering powers in India generally, both ancient and modern, that a kingdom which had submitted should be placed in the charge of some member of its ancient royal family. So both the king of Taxila, who accepted Alexander's summons to submit, and Porus, who valiantly resisted, were made satraps over their own dominions. Indeed, to the former dominions of Porus, who was probably a ruler of exceptional ability, were added those of some of his neighbours.

Thus, in all periods of history, local governments in India have gone on almost unchanged in spite of conquest after conquest. It was always regarded as a legitimate object of the ambition of every king to aim at the position of a *chakravartin* or 'supreme monarch.' If his neighbours agreed, so much the better; but, if they resisted his pretentions, the question was decided by a pitched battle. In either case, the government of the states involved was usually not affected. The same prince continued to rule, and the nature of his rule did not depend on his position as suzerain or vassal king. Generally speaking, the condition of the ordinary people was not affected, or was only affected indirectly, by the victories or defeats of their rulers. The army was not recruited from the tillers of the soil. The soldier was born, not made. It was just as much the duty of certain castes to fight, as it was the duty of others not to fight. War was a special department of government in which the common people had no share.

These considerations enable us to understand why the invasion of India by Alexander the Great has left no traces whatever in the literature or in the institutions of India. It affected no changes either in the methods of government or in the life of the people. It was little more than a military expedition, the main object of which was to gratify a conqueror's ambition by the assertion of his suzerainty. But this suzerainty was only effective so long as it could be enforced. In June 323 B.C., a little more than a year after his return from India, Alexander died at Babylon, and with his death Macedonian rule in India ceased. His successor, Seleucus Nicator, endeavoured in vain to re-conquer the lost possessions, *c.* 305 B.C. Before this date all the states of North-Western India, including whatever remnants there may have been of the military colonies established by Alexander, had come under the sway of an Indian suzerain.

CHAPTER VII

THE MAURYA EMPIRE

The Kingdom of Magadha—Chandragupta—Seleucus Nicator—Megasthenes—Bindusāra—Açoka—His edicts—Extent of the Maurya Empire—Intercourse with the West—The propagation of Buddhism—Later history of the Mauryas—Continuity of policy of Indian rulers.

THE descriptions of Alexander's campaign are especially valuable as enabling us to realize the political conditions of the land of the Indus at this period. We may gather from Indian literature that the political conditions of the land of the Ganges were not widely different. Here, too, the country was divided into a number of states varying greatly in size and power; and here, too, at some period between the lifetime of Buddha and the invasion of Alexander the Great, a conquering power—but, in this case, a native power—had succeeded in establishing a suzerainty over its neighbours. The kingdom of Magadha (S. Bihār) was already growing in power in Buddha's time; and we are probably justified in inferring from the statements of Alexander's historians that its ascendancy over the Prasioi, or the nations of Hindustān, was complete at the time of his invasion.

Soon after the return of Alexander, the throne of Magadha, and with it the imperial possessions of the Nanda dynasty, passed by a *coup d'état* into the hands of an adventurer whom the Greek and Latin writers call Sandrokottos. As we have seen, the identification of this personage with the Chandragupta, who is well known from Indian literature, and whose story, at a later date, formed the subject of a Sanskrit historical play called the *Mudrā-rākshasa*, supplied the first fixed point in the chronology of Ancient India.

Chandragupta, whose surname Maurya is supposed to be derived from the name of his mother, Murā, is the first historical founder of a great empire in India. As king of Magadha he succeeded to a predominant position in Hindustān; and, within a few years of Alexander's departure from India, he had gained possession also of the North-Western region. The empire which he established included therefore the whole of Northern India lying between the Himālaya and Vindhya Mountains, together with that portion of Afghānistān which lies south of the Hindu Kush. We have no detailed information as to the process by which the North-Western region thus passed from one suzerainty to another,

We can only surmise that the victorious career of Chandragupta must have resembled that of Alexander—that some states willingly gave in their allegiance to the new conqueror, while others did not submit without a contest.

Alexander's death in 323 B.C. was followed by a long struggle between his generals for the possession of the empire. The eastern portion which, in theory at least, included the Indian dominions, fell eventually to Seleucus Nicator, who took possession of Babylon and founded the dynasty commonly known as that of the Seleucid Kings of Syria in 312 B.C.

About the year 305 B.C., Seleucus invaded India with the object of reclaiming the conquests of Alexander which had now passed into the power of Chandragupta. No detailed account of this expedition is extant. We only know from Greek and Latin sources that Seleucus crossed the Indus, and that he concluded with Chandragupta a treaty of peace, by the terms of which the Indian provinces formerly held by Darius and Alexander were definitely acknowledged to form part of the empire of Chandragupta.

The most important consequence of this treaty was the establishment of political relations between the kingdom of Syria, which was now the predominant power in Western Asia, and the Maurya empire of Northern India. For a considerable period after this date there is evidence that these political relations were maintained. The Maurya empire was acknowledged in the West as one of the great powers; and ambassadors both from Syria and from Egypt resided at the Maurya capital, Pāṭaliputra (Patna).

The first ambassador sent by Seleucus to the court of Chandragupta was Megasthenes, who wrote an account of India which became the chief source of information for subsequent Greek and Latin authors. The work itself is lost, but numerous fragments of it have been preserved in the form of quotations by later writers.

Among these quotations we find descriptions of very great historical value. The capital, Pāṭaliputra, was, according to Megasthenes, built in the form of a large parallelogram 80 stadia long and 15 stadia wide. That is to say, the city was more than 9 miles in length and more than 1½ miles in width. It was surrounded by a wall which had 570 towers and 64 gates, and by a moat 600 feet wide and 30 cubits deep. At the present time excavations are being made by the Archæological Survey of India on the ancient site of Pāṭaliputra, as the result of which discoveries of the highest interest may be anticipated.

To Megasthenes also we are indebted for a detailed

account of the administration of public affairs in this imperial city; and this account is supplemented and confirmed in a very remarkable manner by a Sanskrit treatise on the conduct of affairs of state, called the *Artha-çāstra*, the authorship of which is attributed to Chāṇakya, who appears as the Brahman prime minister of Chandragupta in the *Mudrā-rākshasa*, and who has won for himself the reputation of having been 'the Machiavelli of India.' It has been well said (V. A. Smith, *Early History of India*, second edition, p. 119), that we are more fully informed concerning political and municipal institutions in the reign of Chandragupta, than in that of any subsequent Indian monarch until the time of the Mughal Emperor Akbar, who was contemporary with our Queen Elizabeth.

The reign of Chandragupta lasted from about 321 to 297 B.C. He was succeeded by a son who is called Bindusāra in Indian literature and who was probably known to Greek writers by one of his titles as Amitrochates (Sanskrit *Amitraghāta*), 'the slayer of his foes.' There is little information to be obtained about him either from Indian or from Greek sources. In his reign another Syrian ambassador named Daimachus, sent by Antiochus I Soter (280-261 B.C.), the successor of Seleucus, visited the court of Pāṭaliputra. He also wrote an account of India, which has been lost. We therefore have no means of judging of the truth of Strabo's statement, when he says that of all the Greek writers on India Daimachus ranked first in mendacity.

Of a third ambassador, who came to India from the West at some time during this period, we know merely the name—Dionysius—and that he was sent from the court of Ptolemy Philadelphus, king of Egypt (285-247 B.C.).

The three ambassadors, whose names have been preserved, are no doubt typical of a class. It is in every way probable that constant relations were maintained between India and the West during the period of the Maurya empire. There is positive evidence of the continuation of such relations during the reign of the next emperor—the most renowned of the imperial line—Açoka, the son of Bindusāra, who reigned *c.* 269-227 B.C.

Açoka's fame rests chiefly on the position which he held as the great patron of Buddhism. As such he has often been compared to Constantine the Great, the royal patron of Roman Christianity. The literary sources for the history of Açoka's reign—Brahman, Jain, and Buddhist—are indeed abundant. But his very fame has, in many cases, caused these materials to assume a legendary or miraculous character. He has suffered both from the enthusiasm of friends and from the misrepresentations of foes. The Buddhist accounts of his life have come down to us in two great collections of religious books—those written in Pali and preserved in Ceylon, and those written in Sanskrit and preserved in Nepāl. In the case of both of these, an undoubted substratum of fact is so much hidden by a dense overgrowth of legend, that the historian is sorely perplexed in his efforts to distinguish the one from the other.

Fortunately, there exists a source of information which is beyond dispute—inscriptions cut into hard rocks or pillars of stone by command of the king himself, and, in many instances, recording his own words. We have already had occasion to speak of these wonderful inscriptions. Their object was ethical and religious rather than historical or political. They inculcate good government among the rulers, and obedience and good conduct among the governed, and these virtues as the fruit of the observance of *dhamma* (Skt. *dharma*) or 'duty,' a term which, in this case, since Açoka was a follower of Buddha, is probably identical with the eight-fold path of Buddhism. In striking contrast to the inscriptions of Darius, the edicts of Açoka were intended not to convey to posterity the record of conquests or of the extent of a mighty empire, but to further the temporal and spiritual welfare of his subjects.

They proclaim in so many words that "the chief conquest is the conquest of 'duty.'" One material conquest—that of the kingdom of Kalinga—they do indeed record; but this is expressly cited as an instance of the worthlessness of conquest by force when compared with the conquest which comes of the performance of 'duty,' and it is coupled with an expression of bitter regret for the destruction and the misery which the war entailed. Surely, imperial edicts of this description, engraved as they are in the most permanent form and promulgated throughout the length and breadth of a great empire, are unique in the history of the world.

Of peculiar interest is the inscribed pillar which was erected by Açoka to mark the traditional birth-place of Buddha. This was discovered in 1896 at Rummindeī in the Nepalese Tarai, with every letter still as perfect as when it was first engraved. The modern name of the place still continues to represent the 'Lumbini' grove of the ancient story of Buddha's birth.

But, although the edicts and the other inscriptions of Açoka are not historical in character, yet they supply, incidentally, evidence of the most valuable kind for the history of the time.

In the first place, the extent of the Maurya empire during the reign of Açoka is indicated by their geographical distribution. They are found, usually at ancient places of pilgrimage, from the N.-W. Frontier Province in the extreme north of India to Mysore in the south, and from Kāthiāwār in the west to Orissa. That is to say, they show that the sway of Açoka extended over the whole length and breadth of the continent of India, with the exception of the extreme south of the peninsula. It is extremely probable also that versions of the edicts will be found in Southern Afghānistān, when it is possible to pursue archæological investigations in that region.

The geographical knowledge thus gleaned is supplemented by the mention in the inscriptions of the peoples living on the northern and southern fringes of the empire. In the north, Açoka regarded his empire as conterminous with that of the Greek (Yona) king Antiochus, that is to say, the Seleucid king, Antiochus II Theos (261-246 B.C.). His neighbours in the extreme south were the rulers of the Tamil kingdoms, four of which are mentioned by name. Three of these kingdoms, which can be identified with certainty, played an important part in later Indian history. The inscriptions also mention Ceylon (Tambapaṇṇi). We are thus, for the first time in the history of India, supplied with information which would enable us to give some description of the geography of the whole continent from Afghānistān to Ceylon.

We also learn incidentally that this great empire was governed by viceroys who ruled over large provinces in the North-West, the South, the East, and the West. The central districts were probably under the direct rule of the emperor at Pāṭaliputra.

We find, further, evidence of the continuance of that intercourse between India and the West, which, as we know from Greek authorities, was maintained during the reigns of Chandragupta and Bindusāra. Açoka was a zealous Buddhist. He was not satisfied with having the 'law of duty' preached everywhere among his subjects and among the independent peoples of Southern India and Ceylon; but he states in one of his edicts that he had sent his missionaries even into the Hellenic kingdoms of Syria, Egypt, Cyrene, Macedonia, and Epirus. He mentions by name the reigning sovereigns of these kingdoms, and thereby supplies some most valuable chronological evidence for the history of his own reign, since the dates of most of these Hellenic kings are known with certainty.

During the reign of Açoka, Buddhism was established in the island of Ceylon, where it still continues to flourish hundreds of years after it has disappeared from every part of the continent of India except Nepāl. The ruler of the island at this period was Tissa (*c.* 247-207 B.C.) whose title *Devānampiya*, 'dear to the gods,' is that which is used by Açoka himself in his inscriptions and may possibly have been borrowed from him. The conversion of the island to Buddhism is attributed by the Ceylonese chronicles to the son of Açoka, Mahinda, who had become a Buddhist monk.

In his latter years the emperor Açoka himself became a monk, living in seclusion at Suvarṇagiri, a sacred mountain, near the ancient city of Girivraja in Magadha (S. Bihār). Like many of the Indian monarchs of old whose story is told in the Sanskrit epics, he retired to devote the final stage of life to religious meditation, after having first transferred the cares of state to his heir apparent. This prince is mentioned in an edict which Açoka issued from Suvarṇagiri, but only by his title. We have no means of identifying him farther, or of knowing if he succeeded to the throne on the death of Açoka.

For the subsequent history of the Maurya empire, we have no such authorities, literary or inscriptional, as those which enable us to understand so fully the social and political conditions of India during the reigns of Chandragupta and

Açoka. We are once more dependent almost entirely on the testimony of the Purāṇas and the chronicles of the Jains and Buddhists—sources which are only partly in agreement with one another, and which at best afford little more than the names of the successors of Açoka and the length of their reigns.

Five of the Purāṇas agree in the statement that the Maurya dynasty lasted for 137 years. If we accept this statement we may date the end of the dynasty in *c.* 184 B.C. They are not in complete agreement either as to the names or the number of Açoka's successors. Two of the Purāṇas agree in stating that his immediate successors were a son and grandson who reigned each for a period of eight years. The latter of these is probably the Daçaratha whose name occurs in some cave-inscriptions in the Nāgārjuni Hills in the Gayā district of Bengal. These inscriptions show that Daçaratha had continued the patronage which Açoka had bestowed on a sect of Jain ascetics called Ājīvikas.

It is possible that the Purāṇas may be right in recording that some six or seven successors of Açoka sat on the throne of Magadha ; but, if so, it is certain that most of these successors could only have ruled over an empire very greatly diminished in extent or, perhaps, even reduced to the kingdom of Magadha out of which it had grown.

It is interesting in reviewing the past history of India to trace a remarkable continuity of policy on the part of the rulers of whatever nationality who have succeeded in welding together this great congeries of widely differing races and tongues. The main principles of government have remained unchanged throughout the ages. Such as they were under the Maurya empire, so they were inherited by the Muhammadan rulers and by their successors the British. These principles are based on the recognition of a social system which depends ultimately on a self-organized village community. Local government thus forms the very basis of all political systems in India. The grouping of village communities into states, and the grouping of states into empires has left the social system unchanged. All governments have been obliged to recognize an infinite variety among the governed of social customs and of religious beliefs, too firmly grounded to admit of interference. Thus the idea of religious toleration which was of slow growth in Europe was accepted in India generally from the earliest times. All religious communities were alike under the protection of the sovereign; and inscriptions plainly show that, when the government changed hands, the privileges granted to religious communities were ratified by the new sovereign as a matter of course. In a special edict devoted to the subject of religious toleration Açoka definitely says that his own practice was to reverence all sects. In this edict he deprecates the habit of exalting one's own views at the expense of others, and admits that different people have different ideas as to what constitutes 'duty' (*dharma*). Such has been the attitude of enlightened rulers of India in all ages. Instances of religious persecution have, indeed, not been wanting in India; but the tolerant policy of Açoka was that of the most capable and far-seeing of the Muhammadan rulers such as Akbar, and it has always been that of the British government, which, like Açoka, has only interfered with religion when it has entailed practices which conflict with the ordinary principles of humanity.

CHAPTER VIII

INDIA AFTER THE DECLINE OF THE MAURYA EMPIRE

Dismemberment of the Empire—The Çuṅgas—The Kingdom of Kaliṅga—The Andhras—The Hellenic Kingdoms of Bactria and Parthia—The Indian invasion of Antiochus the Great.

ANOTHER lesson which is enforced by the history of the Maurya empire is that the maintenance of peace, and of those conditions which are essential to progress, depends in India on the existence of a strong imperial power. On the downfall of the Maurya empire, as on the downfall of the Mughal empire nearly two thousand years later, the individual states which had been peacefully united under the imperial sway regained their independence, and the struggle between them for existence or for supremacy began anew. The literature and the monuments afford us some information as to the history of various regions of India during the period of strife and confusion which now ensued.

According to the Purāṇas the Mauryas were

succeeded on the throne of Magadha by the Çuṅgas who are said to have ruled for 112 years (*c.* 184-72 B.C.). There is no reason to disbelieve this statement which is consonant with probability and with such other evidence as we possess; but, after this period, it seems impossible to make the chronology of the Purāṇas agree with the more trustworthy evidence of inscriptions and coins. In this case it seems probable that the dynastic lists were originally authentic, but that later editors have reduced them to absurdity by representing contemporary dynasties as successive.

The founder of the Çuṅga dynasty was Pushyamitra who is said to have slain his master, Bṛihadratha, the last of the royal Mauryas. An historical play, the *Mālavikāgnimitra*, by India's greatest dramatist, Kālidāsa, who flourished *c.* 400 A.D., deals with this period. Although a composition of this kind, written between five and six centuries after the date of the events to which it refers, cannot be accepted as historical evidence, yet it is altogether probable that its chief characters—Pushyamitra, his son Agnimitra, and his grandson Vasumitra—were historical personages, and that some of the events mentioned—a war with Vidarbha (Berār) and a conflict with the Yavanas, for instance—were actual occurrences. The picture of a diminished empire still possessed by Magadha is in accordance with the knowledge of the period which we derive from more trustworthy sources. The king probably still reigned at the capital, Pāṭaliputra, while his son, the heir-apparent, like Açoka before he came to the throne, governed the western provinces with his court at Vidiçā (Bhīlsa) in Mālwā (Central India). It was before the vice-regal court of the same province and at its capital, Ujjain, that the play was first performed during the reign of the later Gupta emperor, Chandragupta II Vikramāditya (*c.* 375-413 A.D.).

The extent of the Çuṅga dominions is indicated by an inscription 'in the sovereignty of the Çuṅga kings' which occurs on one of the sculptures from the Bhārhut tope in the Nāgod State (Central India), and possibly also by certain coins found in the United Provinces in Rohilkhand, the ancient kingdom of North Pañchāla, and on the site of Ayodhyā, the ancient capital of Kosala (Oudh); but the names found on these coins, with the single exception of 'Agnimitra,' only bear a general resemblance with those given in the dynastic lists and cannot be identified with certainty.

The available evidence thus tends to show that Magadha under the Çuṅgas still possessed an empire, but one greatly reduced in size since the time of Açoka. Some of the losses which the empire had sustained are clearly proved by the evidence of inscriptions and coins.

The kingdom of Kaliṅga, on the east coast between the rivers Mahānadī and Godāvarī, had, as we know from Açoka's edicts, been conquered by him in the ninth year after his coronation. It would seem to have regained its independence at no long interval after his death, according to evidence supplied by an inscription of Khāravela, king of Kaliṅga, in the Hāthigumphā cave near Cuttack in Orissa. Unfortunately, the inscription, which gives an account of events in the first thirteen years of the king's reign, is much damaged, and its interpretation is full of difficulties. What appears to be beyond all doubt is the statement that Khāravela belonged to the third generation of the royal family of Kaliṅga. The mention of an Andhra king, Çātakarṇi, and such other chronological indications as can be obtained from the inscription, would seem to suggest that Khāravela was reigning *c.* 150 B.C. No more precise date is obtainable at present.

The decline of the Maurya empire was marked also by the rapid growth of the Andhra kingdom in Southern India. Originally a Dravidian people living immediately to the south of the Kaliṅgas in that part of the Madras Presidency which lies between the rivers Godāvarī and Kistna, the

Andhras had become, probably about 200 B.C., a great power whose territories included the whole of the Deccan and extended to the western coast. They are mentioned in the edicts in a manner which seems to indicate that they acknowledged the suzerainty of Açoka, but that they were never conquered and brought under the direct government of a viceroy of the empire like their neighbours the Kaliṅgas. They would seem to have asserted their independence soon after the death of Açoka. Some outline of their history may be traced by the aid of inscriptions, coins, and literary sources from probably about 220 B.C. to 240 A.D. The names of a succession of thirty kings are preserved in the Purāṇas, together with the length of each reign, and the total duration of the dynasty which is given either as 456 or as 460 years. The Purāṇas are, usually, fairly in agreement with the evidence of inscriptions and coins, so far as the names of the kings and the length of their reigns are concerned; but they assign to the dynasty a chronological position which is impossible.

There can be little doubt also that, contemporaneously with the rise of the independent kingdoms of the Kaliṅgas and the Andhras in the South, the North-Western region of India, too, ceased to belong to the Maurya empire. We have no glimpses of the history of this defection; but we may reasonably assume that the numerous petty states which had been held together for a time by the imperial power reasserted their autonomy when that power ceased.

During the reign of Açoka two revolts occurred in the empire of Syria which were fruitful in consequences for the future history of India. Almost at the same time, about 250 B.C. or a few years later, Diodotus, satrap of Bactria, and a Parthian adventurer named Arsaces threw off their allegiance to the Seleucid monarch, Antiochus II Theos (261-246 B.C.), and founded the independent kingdoms of Bactria and Parthia.

Bactria—the name is preserved in the modern form *Balkh*—was the region of N. Afghānistān, bounded on the north by the river Oxus. It was divided from the Maurya empire by the Hindu Kush—a range of mountains which, lofty as are many of its peaks, possesses also numerous passes, and forms no very formidable barrier to communication between Northern and Southern Afghānistān. The Hellenic kingdom of Bactria founded by Diodotus lasted till about 135 B.C., when its civilization was entirely swept away by the irresistible flood of Scythian (Çaka) invasion from the North. Its brief history of a little more than a century is most intimately associated with that of the North-Western region of India.

Parthia, originally a province lying to the south-east of the Caspian Sea, grew into a great empire at the expense of the empire of Syria, which, once the predominant power in Western Asia, was at last reduced to the province of Syria from which it takes its name. The Parthian power lasted till 226 A.D. In the reign of Mithradates I (171-138 B.C.) it extended as far eastwards as the river Indus which thus became once more the dividing line between Western Asia and India. The Parthian and Scythian invasions of India, which, at a somewhat later period, constitute the chief feature in the history of the North-Western region are dealt with in our final chapter.

But the Syrian empire did not acquiesce without a protest in the independence of its revolted provinces. About the year 209 B.C., Antiochus III the Great, made an attempt to reduce both Parthia and Bactria to obedience. Parthia was now under the rule of the king who has usually, but perhaps incorrectly, been called Artabanus I (210-191 B.C.), while Bactria was under Euthydemus (*c.* 230-195 B.C.). The expedition of Antiochus ended in an acknowledgement of the independence of both kingdoms. So far as Bactria is concerned, Antiochus is said to have listened to the argument of Euthydemus that it would at the present juncture be impolitic, in the cause of Hellenic civilization generally, to weaken the power of Bactria which formed a barrier against the constant menace of Scythian irruptions from the North.

Bactria was, indeed, a stronghold of Hellenic civilization. It was held by a military aristocracy, thoroughly Greek in sentiment and religion, ruling over a subject people so little advanced in culture that its ideas are in no way reflected in the monuments of Bactrian art. The coins of Bactria are purely Greek in character, the divinities represented on them are Greek, and the portraits of the kings themselves are among the finest examples extant of Greek art as applied to portraiture. But the kingdom was short-lived and its history was troublous. The house of the founder, Diodotus, was deposed by Euthydemus, perhaps about 230 B.C., and the later history of Bactria is occupied with the internecine struggle between the descendants of Euthydemus and the rival family of Eucratides.

After thus making a treaty of peace with Euthydemus, Antiochus, like his predecessors, Alexander in 327 B.C., and Seleucus *c.* 305 B.C.

passed over the Hindu Kush into the Kābul Valley. No exact details of this invasion or of its extent have been preserved; but it seems clear that this region, which formed part of the Maurya empire when Seleucus invaded it, had, at some time subsequent to the death of Açoka, reverted to the rule of its local princes, one of whom, Sophagasenus (probably the Sanskrit *Subhagasena*), is said to have purchased peace by offering tribute to Antiochus.

CHAPTER IX

THE SUCCESSORS OF ALEXANDER THE GREAT

The records literary and numismatic—Bactrian conquests in India—Invasion of Bactria by Mithradates—Bactria occupied by the Çakas and the Yueh-chi—Greek kings in India—The house of Euthydemus and the house of Eucratides—Menander—Allusions to Greeks in Sanskrit literature—Greek influence in India.

THE political condition of India on the downfall of the Maurya empire was such as to invite foreign invasion; and the establishment on its northern and north-western borders of the kingdoms of Bactria and Parthia supplied the sources from which invasions came.

The literary authorities for the history of this period are indeed few; but they afford some most valuable information. The most important are:—(1) Justin, a Latin writer who, in the fourth or fifth century A.D., made an abridgement of a history of the Macedonian empire compiled by Trogus in the reign of Augustus (27 B C.-14 A.D.); and (2) the Greek geographer Strabo, who was probably contemporary with Trogus.

The chief records, however, of the rulers of this period are their coins, which are found in extraordinary variety and abundance. From them we learn of the existence of thirty-five kings and two queens, all bearing purely Greek names, who reigned in Bactria and India during the period from about 250 B.C. to 25 B.C. The great majority of these rulers are otherwise unknown. The coins which they struck have survived, while every other memorial of their lives has perished. A curious fact connected with this series of coins is that certain specimens struck in Bactria before 200 B.C. are of nickel, a metal which is commonly supposed to have been discovered in Europe about the middle of the eighteenth century A.D.

Not long after the expedition ot Antiochus the Great, the Bactrian king Euthydemus seems to have formed the design of extending his kingdom by the conquest of the territories lying to the south of the Hindu Kush. It is probable that the fulfilment of this design was entrusted to his son Demetrius, who has been supposed to be the original of

> 'The grete Emetreus, the king of Inde'

of Chaucer's *Knightes Tale*.

As a result of the conquests of Demetrius, the ancient provinces of the Persian empire, *i.e.* the

Kābul Valley and the country of the Indus (the Western Punjab and Sind), which had been once reclaimed and held for a brief period by Alexander the Great, were now again recovered for the Greek kings of Bactria who proudly boasted to be his successors.

But though Demetrius had thus gained a new kingdom in India, he was soon to lose his own kingdom of Bactria after a desperate struggle with his rival Eucratides, who now laid claim to the throne. The account of an episode in this contest has been preserved by Justin, who describes how Eucratides with 300 men was besieged by Demetrius with 60,000, and how he wore out the enemy by continual sorties and escaped in the fifth month of the siege. Finally, not only Bactria but also some part of the newly acquired Indian dominions of Demetrius passed into the power of the conqueror, Eucratides; and from this time onwards we may trace the existence of two lines of Greek princes in India, the one derived from Euthydemus, ending *c.* 100 B.C., and the other derived from Eucratides, ending *c.* 25 B.C.

The period of the reign of Eucratides is determined by the statement of Justin that he came to the throne at about the same time as Mithradates I of Parthia, *i.e.* about 171 B.C. It is doubtful if Demetrius or any other member of the family of Euthydemus ruled in any part of Bactria after this date. It is more probable that henceforth their power was confined to India. The family of Eucratides, on the other hand, continued to rule both in Bactria and in India until Greek civilization in Bactria was swept away by the flood of Çaka invasions from the North *c.* 135 B.C.; but they retained their possessions in the territories to the south of the Hindu Kush, and held the Kābul Valley until the Kushāṇa conquest, *c.* 25 B.C.

The transference of Greek rule from Bactria to India is indicated, in the most unmistakable manner, by a change in the style of the coins. In Bactria the coins remain purely Greek in character, and they are struck in accordance with a purely Greek standard of weight. The subject population was evidently not sufficiently advanced in civilization to influence the art of the conquerors in any degree. In India, on the other hand, where the Greeks came into contact with an ancient civilization, which was, in many respects, as advanced as their own, it was necessary to effect a compromise. It was essential that the coinage should be suited to the requirements of the conquered as well as of the conquerors. The coins, accordingly, become bilingual. They are struck with Greek legends on the *obverse*, and with an Indian translation in Indian characters on the *reverse*; and they follow the Persian standard of weight which had been firmly established in N.-W. India as a result of the long Persian dominion. We have already seen how valuable the study of these bilingual coins has proved in affording the necessary clue to the interpretation of the forgotten alphabets of Ancient India.

During the reign of Eucratides, Bactria was invaded by the Parthian king, Mithradates I (171-138 B.C.), who seems to have remained master of the country for some considerable time. It is probable that certain coins which bear his name, and which are palpably imitated, some from the Bactrian coins of Demetrius and some from those of Eucratides, may have been struck by him in Bactria during this period. There is reason for supposing that Mithradates, on this occasion, penetrated even into India. In the printed text of the works of Orosius, a Roman historian who flourished *c.* 400 A.D., there is indeed to be found a definite statement to the effect that Mithradates subdued the nations between the Hydaspes (Jhelum) and the Indus; but it seems possible that the reading 'Hydaspes' may be incorrect and due to some corruption in the manuscripts of the name of a river not in India, but in Persia to the west of the Indus.

Thus weakened, on the one hand, by internal feuds and by Parthian attacks, and, on the other, by the drain on its resources caused by the Indian conquests, the Greek kingdom of Bactria proved incapable of resisting the hordes of Scythians who burst through its northern frontiers *c.* 135 B.C. These represented one of the groups of nomadic tribes known as Çakas, who still occupied, as in the time of Darius (522-486 B.C.), the country of the river Jaxartes (Syr Darya) to the north of Sogdiāna (Bukhāra). They had always been regarded as a standing menace to the Greek civilization of Bactria, and now, being driven from their pastures by the pressure of other nomadic hordes whom the Chinese historians call Yueh-chi, they were forced partly in a southerly direction into Bactria, and partly in a south-westerly direction into the Parthian empire where they joined with an earlier settlement of Çakas in the province of Drangiāna (Seistān). Traces of the existence of this earlier Çaka settlement in Drangiāna seem to be found both in the inscriptions of Darius and in the accounts of Alexander's campaigns. The vital importance for the history of N.-W. India of this augmentation of the Çaka power already established in a province of the Parthian Empire will be seen subsequently (p. 137).

The Yueh-chi, thus driving the Çakas before

them, seem to have occupied first Sogdiāna and then Bactria, where, under the leadership of their chief tribe, the Kushāṇas, they developed into the strong power which created the next great Indian empire.

It is only possible to give a very general outline of the history of the Greek kingdoms south of the Hindu Kush. Nearly all the evidence which we possess has been gleaned from the study of their coinages; and the interpretation of this evidence is by no means always clear. As has been observed, these Greek princes seem to belong chiefly to the two rival royal lines—the house of Euthydemus, and the house of Eucratides—which having begun their struggle in Bactria continued it in India. It is, however, not always easy to attribute princes whose coins we possess to either of these groups; and it is quite possible that, in addition to these two chief Greek kingdoms in Northern India, there may have been other principalities which Greek soldiers of fortune had carved out for themselves.

The Indian conquests of Demetrius, the son of Euthydemus, were greatly extended by later rulers of the same house, notably by Apollodotus and Menander. That these two princes were intimately connected there can be no doubt. They use the same coin-types, especially the figure of the Greek goddess, Athene, hurling the thunderbolt, which is characteristic of other members of the family of Euthydemus, *e.g.* the Stratos; and they are twice mentioned together in literature. Strabo attributes conquests in India to them jointly, while the unknown author of the *Periplus maris Erythrai*—a most interesting handbook intended for the use of Greek merchants and seamen as a guide to the coasting voyage from the Persian Gulf to the west coast of India—states that small silver coins, inscribed with Greek characters and bearing the names of these two princes, were still current in his time (probably *c.* 80 A.D.) at the port of Barugaza (Broach). The extent of Menander's dominions especially is indicated both by the great variety of his coin-types which prove that he ruled over a great number of different provinces, and by a statement quoted by Strabo to the effect that he passed beyond the Hyphasis (Beās) which formed the extreme limit of Alexander's conquests.

We have, in all probability, further information concerning Menander from a source which, at first sight, might seem not very promising from the point of view of the historian. Menander is almost certainly to be identified with the King Milinda, who is known from a Buddhist philosophical treatise called the 'Questions of Milinda'

(*Milinda-Pañha*). This monarch resided at Çākala, an ancient city which has been identified with the modern Siālkot in the N.E. Punjab. Now, we have direct evidence that other members of the house of Euthydemus (the Stratos) reigned to the S.E. of the Punjab, since their coins are imitated by their Çaka conquerors who occupied the district of Mathurā (Muttra). We may conclude, then, that the family of Euthydemus ruled over the E. Punjab, with one of its capitals at Siālkot and possibly another capital in the Muttra Dist. of the United Provinces.

But the evidence both of coins and of literature shows that, at one period, they possessed a far wider dominion. The fact that the coins of Apollodotus and Menander were current at Broach, surely indicates that their conquests must have extended to Western India (Gujarāt and Kāthiāwār); while the statement in Strabo, that Menander passed beyond the Beās into the Middle Country, is supported by certain references in Sanskrit literature to the warlike activity of the Yavanas (Greeks) about the middle of the second century B.C. The best known of these allusions are the following:—

(1) Kālidāsa's historical play, the *Mālavikāgnimitra*, represents the forces of the first Çunga king, Pushyamitra, under the command of his grandson, Vasumitra, as coming into conflict with

the Yavanas somewhere in Central India. This may well be the reminiscence of some episode in Menander's invasion of the Çuṅga dominions.

(2) The grammarian Patañjali, in his *Mahābhāshya* or 'Great Commentary' on Pāṇini's Sanskrit Grammar, mentions King Pushyamitra as if he were his contemporary, and refers to the sieges by the Yavanas of Sāketa in South Oudh and of Madhyamikā (Nāgarī) near Chitor in Rājputāna as if they had taken place within his own memory.

(3) Perhaps the fullest of all the accounts of the Greeks in India at this period occurs in an astronomical, or rather astrological, treatise called the *Gārgī Saṃhitā*, or 'the compendium of Garga.' One of its chapters is in the style of a Purāṇa; that is to say, it gives in a prophetic form an account of kings who have already ruled on the earth. Unfortunately this work has not yet been fully edited and the manuscript of it which has been described is both fragmentary and corrupt. Put into historic form the information which the certain portions of this chapter yield may be expressed as follows:—

The Greeks after reducing Sāketa, the Pañchāla country and Muttra (all in the United Provinces) reached the capital Pāṭaliputra (Patna). But they did not stay in the Middle Country because of the strife between themselves which took place in their own kingdom (North-Western India). They were eventually conquered by a Çaka king; and in time the Çakas yielded to another conquering power, the name of which is obscured by textual corruption in the manuscript.

This account no doubt refers successively to the internecine struggle between the house of Euthydemus and the house of Eucratides, to the conquest of Greek kingdoms by the Çakas, and to the subsequent conquest of the Çakas by the Kushāṇas. The Gārgī Saṃhitā holds an almost unique position in the literature of Ancient India, and it is much to be regretted that no edition of this interesting work is at present possible. It is almost the only surviving representative of the old Hindu astrology or astronomy, which was superseded, probably in the fourth century A.D., by the Greek system of astronomy borrowed, presumably, from Alexandria. The later Indian astronomers frequently refer to Vṛiddha Garga, 'the old Garga,' and there is no reason to doubt that the compendium which bears his name belongs to a period not much later than that of the foreign invaders whom it mentions. The information conveyed by the chapter to which we have referred is in accordance with the knowledge of this period which we may glean independently from other sources.

The territories on the extreme north-western frontier of India, *i.e.* the Kābul Valley and Gandhāra (including Taxila) which were originally conquered by Euthydemus or by Demetrius, were wrested from this family of Greek princes by Eucratides. Evidence of the transfer of this region from one rule to the other is afforded by certain coins which have been restruck. Originally they were issued by Apollodotus, a prince of the house of Euthydemus; but they have been restruck by Eucratides; and, as they bear the image and superscription of the tutelary deity of Kāpiça, the capital city of Gandhāra, they testify to the change of government which had taken place in this province.

Inscriptions and coins show further that the family of Eucratides was supplanted by Çaka satraps in both Kāpiça and Taxila; but these princes continued to hold the Kābul Valley until the last vestiges of their rule, which had survived the attacks of the Çakas, were swept away by the Kushāṇas. The last Greek king to reign in the Kābul Valley, and indeed in any region of India, was Hermæus who was succeeded, *c.* 25 A.D., by the Kushāṇa chief, Kujūla Kadphises.

It is a curious fact that, while the coinages of the Græco-Indian princes are remarkably abundant, all other memorials of their rule should be so rare. Only one stone inscription, for instance, has yet been found in which any of these princes is mentioned. This inscription is at Besnagar in Gwalior, and the prince mentioned is Antialcidas who, to judge from the evidence of coins, was one of the earlier members of the line of Eucratides, and who ruled both in Bactria and in the Kābul Valley. The inscription records the erection of a standard in honour of the god Vishṇu; and it is especially interesting as showing that the donor, a Greek named Heliodorus, the son of Dion, who had come to Besnagar as an ambassador from Antialcidas, had adopted an Indian faith. The inscription is dated in the 14th year of the reign of a king Bhāgabhadra who presumably ruled over the province in which Besnagar was situated. As this region no doubt formed part of the empire of the Çuṅgas, it is not improbable that this King Bhāgabhadra may be identical with the Bhadra or Bhadraka who is mentioned in some of the Purāṇas among the successors of Pushyamitra.

It is to the period of nearly two centuries (*c.* 200-25 B.C.) during which Greek princes ruled in the Kābul Valley, the North-Western Frontier Province, and the Punjab, and not to the expedition of Alexander the Great (327-5 B.C.), the political results of which lasted only for a few

PLATE III.

THE BESNAGAR COLUMN. [*See page* 156.

years, that we must trace the chief source of Greek influence in Northern India. For some centuries after the extinction of all their political power, we find Greeks mentioned in Indian literature and Indian inscriptions. But they have been absorbed into the Indian social system. They bear Indian or Persian names, and they profess Indian faiths. The existence of a strong Greek element in the population is attested by the Buddhist art of Gandhāra, in which the influence of Greek traditions is manifest; and a system of writing developed from the Greek alphabet is to be traced in this region until at least the fourth century A.D., and possibly much later.

CHAPTER X

PARTHIAN AND SCYTHIAN INVADERS

Çakas and Pahlavas—Their Parthian Origin—Progress of Çaka conquests in India—Çaka satrapies—Defeat of the Çakas by a king of Mālwā and the establishment of the Vikrama era—Gondopharnes—Progress of Kushāṇa power Establishment of the Kushāṇa empire — The era of Kanishka.

So far, we have traced the history of the Yavanas (Yonas), or foreign invaders of Greek descent, in North-Western India. The history of this region is now complicated by the appearance on the scene of invaders belonging to two other nationalities, who are constantly associated with the Yavanas in Indian literature and inscriptions. These are the Çakas and Pahlavas.

Herodotus expressly states that the term 'Çakas' was used by the Persians to denote Scythians generally; and this statement is certainly in accordance with the use of the word in the inscriptions of Darius. In one of these, it occurs together with descriptions which show that it denotes certain Scythians in Europe as well as two branches of Scythians in Asia. These, we have reason to believe, are specimens merely of the innumerable swarms of nomads which had been finding their way during untold centuries from that great hive of humanity, China, to Western Asia and to Europe.

The settlements of Çakas which affected the history of India at this period are two in number. One of these occupied the country of the Jaxartes to the north of Bactria and Sogdiāna, and had for ages past been regarded as a great danger to Persian and Hellenic civilization in Central Asia; while the other inhabited the province of Drangiāna, which lay between Persia and India, and which subsequently bore the name of Çakasthāna, 'the abode of the Çakas' (the later Sijistān and the modern Seistān). It is probable that both of these bodies of Çakas were stirred into activity in the middle of the second century B.C. by the same cause—the impact of further swarms of nomads who are known as the Yueh-chi. The result of this impact was two-fold. On the one hand, the Hellenic kingdom of Bactria was submerged in a flood of barbarian invasion, and, on the other, the Parthian kings were occupied during two reigns (Phraates II, 138-128 B.C., and Artabanus II (I), 128-123 B.C.) in endeavours to stem the tide which had extended to Seistān, and were only completely successful in the following reign (Mithradates II the Great, 123-88 B.C.). The effect of the Çaka invasion of the Parthian kingdom was thus to increase the power of a Çaka settlement which was already established in the Parthian province of Seistān, and the result of the struggles between Çakas and Parthians in this region was the creation of a kingdom, probably more or less dependent on the kingdom of Parthia, in which the two peoples were associated.

The third class of foreign invaders, who are, in Indian literature and inscriptions, called Pahlavas, were Parthians, the two names being etymologically identical. It is clear, however, that the Pahlavas who invaded India did not belong to the main stock which was represented by the rulers of the Parthian empire, but rather to the subordinate branch which was established in its eastern provinces, Drangiāna (Seistān), Arachosia (Kandahār) and Gedrosia (Northern Baluchistān). The history of this subordinate kingdom is obscure. Almost our only evidence for its existence is supplied by coins; but these give us names of rulers which are undoubtedly Parthian in character, and the area over which the coins are found affords some indication of the extent of territory which these princes governed. They may have been originally satraps of the Parthian monarchs; but the title 'King of Kings' which, in imitation of their former over-lords, they bear on their coins, shows that they had asserted their independence. The first of these Pahlavas to appear on the coins has the familiar Parthian name Vonones; and we may, therefore, conveniently call the line to which he belongs 'the family of Vonones.'

With this line of Pahlava princes the Çaka invaders of India are intimately connected. Like them, and unlike the Græco-Indian princes, they bear the title 'King of Kings.' The history of this title is interesting. It denoted originally the supreme lord who claimed the allegiance of a number of subordinate kings. It was the ancient title of the Persian monarchs, and as such it appears in the inscriptions of Darius in the form *Kshāyathiyānām Kshāyathiya*. In the Parthian monarchy it seems to occur first on coins of Mithradates II (123-88 B.C.), though some numismatists prefer to attribute the coins in question to Mithradates I (171-138 B.C.). It was introduced into India by the Çaka and Pahlava invaders, and continued in use by their successors, the Kushāṇas; and in the form *Shāhan-shāh* it remains the title of the Shāhs of Persia even to the present day.

There can be no doubt, then, that the distinctive title 'King of Kings' connects the

Indian Çakas with the Pahlavas and both with Parthia; and this connexion is most naturally explained on the theory that these Çakas came into India from Seistān through Kandahār, over the Bolān Pass, through Baluchistān into Sind and so up the valley of the Indus. This would explain the fact that the coins of Maues, the earliest known of these Çaka princes, are found in the Punjab only and not in the Kābul Valley, which still continued to be held by the Greek princes of the family of Eucratides. Access into the Kābul Valley from Bactria over the passes of the Hindu Kush was thus, at this period, barred.

The progress which the Çaka conquests made at the expense of both the chief lines of Greek rulers is illustrated by the coins. Maues strikes coins which are directly imitated from those of Demetrius; the Çaka satrap Liaka Kusūlaka at Taxila imitates the coins of Eucratides, and another satrap, Rañjubula, at Muttra the coins struck by Strato I and II reigning conjointly. Everywhere, indeed, the Çaka invaders seem to have retained the form of coinage used by the Greek princes whom they dispossessed—a coinage distinguished by a Greek legend on the *obverse* and a Prakrit translation in Kharoshṭhī characters on the *reverse*—and it is probable that they only issued coins in those districts where they found a currency already in existence. So far as is known, none of their coinages is original. All without exception are imitated from Greek or Hindu models.

The Çakas continued in North-Western India the system of government by satraps which was firmly established there during the long period of Persian rule. This system was, as we have seen, followed by Alexander the Great, and there is no reason to suppose that it had been interrupted either under the Maurya empire or under the rule of the later Greek princes.

Of the history of these Çaka satrapies inscriptions and coins give us a few details.

An inscription affords the bare mention of a satrap of Kāpiça, the capital of Gandhāra, a district which, as we know from coins, had passed from the family of Euthydemus (Apollodotus) into the power of Eucratides.

There is a copper-plate inscription of a satrap of Taxila named Pātika which records the deposit of relics of the Buddha and a donation made in the 78th year of some era not specified and during the reign of the Great King Moga, who is without doubt to be identified with Maues, since *Moga* is merely a dialectical variant of *Moa*, the Indian equivalent of the name Maues found on the coins. The era in which the inscription is dated cannot at present be determined. The most plausible conjecture is that it may be of Parthian origin; and if it could be supposed to start from the beginning of the reign of Mithradates I (171 B.C.), the monarch who raised Parthia from a comparatively small state to a great empire, which extended from the Euphrates to Bactria and the borders of India, the result as applied to this inscription (171 − 78 = 93 B.C.), would give a date which is fairly probable on other considerations. But it must be admitted that there is no evidence of the existence of such an era. The satrap Pātika was the son of Liaka Kusūlaka, who struck coins imitated from those of Eucratides. It would seem, then, that Taxila, like Kāpiça (Gandhāra), was taken by the Çakas from the family of Eucratides, while the Kābul Valley remained in its possession.

Of the Çaka satraps of Mathurā (Muttra) we possess a most valuable monument, which was discovered and first published by a distinguished Indian scholar, Pandit Bhagvānlāl Indrājī, who bequeathed it together with his valuable collection of ancient Indian coins to the British Museum. It is in the form of a large lion carved in red sandstone and intended to be the capital of a pillar. The workmanship shows undoubted Persian influence. The surface is completely

PLATE IV.

THE MATHURĀ LION-CAPITAL.

[See page 153

covered with inscriptions in Kharoshṭhī characters, which give the genealogy of the satrapal family ruling at Muttra and also mention members of other satrapal houses in other provinces of North-Western India. These inscriptions show that the satraps of Muttra, like those of Kāpiça and Taxila, were Buddhists. The reigning satrap, or rather 'great satrap,' Rājūla (whose name appears also as Rājuvula or Rañjubula) also struck coins, some of which are imitated from the currency of certain Greek princes of the house of Euthydemus—the Stratos—while others are copied from the coins of a line of Hindu princes who ruled at Muttra. We know, therefore, that in this district Çaka rule superseded that of both Greek and Hindu princes.

Evidence of the existence of a Çaka power in Central India and of its defeat by a Hindu king is supplied by a Jain work called the *Kālikāchārya-kathā* or 'story of Kālikāchārya.' From it we learn that the Çakas, who in Mālwā were patrons of the Jain religion, were subdued by a king named Vikramāditya who reigned at Ujjain, and who established the era, beginning in 58 B.C., which still bears his name. The name of the king may, no doubt, be legendary; or possibly, while the name itself has been lost, one of the king's titles, 'the sun of valour,' has survived; but that this era was really first used in Mālwā is probable on other grounds. At a later date (405 A.D.) it is certainly described as 'the traditional reckoning of the Mālava tribe.' The story goes on to say that this era continued in use for 135 years, when it was superseded by one which was founded by another Çaka conqueror. This second era is undoubtedly that which begins in 78 A.D., and it is still called the Çaka era. It is probable further that, soon after the date of its foundation, the Kushāṇa empire extended to Mālwā, and that its conquest was effected by the Pahlava and Çaka satraps of the Kushāṇa emperor, Kanishka (see p. 147).

It has been already observed that there is evidence of an intimate connexion between Pahlavas and Çakas, *i.e.* between 'the family of Vonones' and 'the family of Maues.' This connexion appears to be proclaimed by certain coins on which Spalirises, 'the brother of the king' (*i.e.* presumably of Vonones) is definitely associated with Azes, who was almost certainly the successor of Maues. Such evidence as there is would seem to indicate that these two lines continued to rule over adjacent provinces—the family of Vonones in Seistān, Kandahār, and North Baluchistān, and the family of Maues in the West Punjab and Sind—until, probably towards the end of the first quarter of the first century A.D., the two kingdoms were united under the sway of the Pahlava Gondopharnes, as to the Parthian character of whose name there can be no possible doubt. The evidence is almost entirely numismatic, and its bearings may be summarized as follows. The numerous varieties of the coinage of this monarch, copied as they are from so many previous issues, show that he ruled over a very extensive dominion; and the fact that these varieties are imitated from the currencies both of the family of Vonones and the family of Maues, leads us to the conclusion that he ruled over both the earlier kingdoms of the Pahlavas and of the Çakas.

The fame of King Gondopharnes (or Gondopherres, as the name appears in the Greek coin-legends) spread even to the West, and he is known in the legends of the early Christian Church as the king to whose country St Thomas was sent as the apostle of the 'Parthians,' or, according to other authorities, of the 'Indians,' *i.e.* the people of the Indus country. The story of the mission of St Thomas and of the king's conversion to the Christian faith is told in the apocryphal *Acts of St Thomas*, of which there are extant versions in Syriac, Greek, and Latin, the earliest of these, the Syriac, belonging probably to the third century A.D. Doubtless there must be a great deal in this story which can only be regarded as pure legend, but it is reasonable to suppose that it may have some basis in fact.

The names of several successors of Gondopharnes are known from their coins; but these coins show that they ruled over a greatly diminished realm. Already at this period—the early part of the first century A.D.—the Kushāṇa power, which had grown up in Bactria, had begun to absorb the various states of North-Western India, and to weld together Greeks, Çakas, Pahlavas, and Hindus into one great empire.

The first step in the creation of this Indian empire was the conquest of the last remaining stronghold of Greek rule in the Kābul Valley. The coins show clearly the process by which this region, probably in the last quarter of the first century B.C., passed from Hermæus, the last ruling member of the line of Eucratides, to his conqueror, the Kushāṇa Kujūla Kadphises. The conquest of 'India,' the country of the Indus, was the work of his successor, who is known from his coins as Wima Kadphises, and after him the Kushāṇa empire reached its culminating point in the reign of Kanishka.

The question of the date of Kanishka is still the subject of keen controversy; but it will probably be settled within a short time by the excavations which are now being made by the Archæological Survey of India on the ancient site of Taxila, one of his capitals.

In the meantime, until absolute certainty can be attained, a probable view appears to be that he was the founder of the Çaka era, the initial year of which is 78 A.D., and that the era obtained its name from the fact that it became most widely known in India as that which was used for more than three centuries by the Çaka kings of Surāshṭra (Gujarāt and Kāthiāwār) who were originally satraps and feudatories of the Kushāṇas.

With the establishment of the Kushāṇa Empire we must bring our survey of 'Ancient India' to a close. The history of the remaining ten centuries which elapsed before the Muhammadan period may, perhaps, be more fittingly included under the heading 'Medieval India.' In Medieval, as in Ancient, India we may see the rise and fall of empires, partly of foreign and partly of native origin, some of them the result of invasions through the 'Gates of India' on the north or north-west, others the outcome of the struggle for supremacy between the nationalities of the continent itself.

NOTES ON THE ILLUSTRATIONS

THE GIRNAR ROCK IN 1869

(Plate I, Frontispiece, and Plate V A, facing p. 150)

GIRNĀR, the Sanskrit *Girinagara*, the 'Hill City,' was in ancient times the name of Junāgadh in Kāthiāwār. It is now applied to the sacred mountain on the east of the city. At the foot of this mountain stands a rock which is without question one of the most interesting and valuable of all historical monuments. It is about twelve feet in height and seventy-five feet in circumference at the base; and it has engraved on its surface records of three kings belonging to three different dynasties which have ruled over Western India:—(1) Açoka, the Maurya Emperor, *c.* 250 B.C.; (2) Rudradāman, the Mahākshatrapa or 'Great Satrap' of Surāshṭra and Mālava (inscription dated in the year 72 of what was called at a later date the Çaka era = 150 A.D.); and (3) Skandagupta, the Gupta Emperor (inscription bearing dates in the years 136, 137, and 138 of the Gupta era beginning in 319 A.D. = 455, 456, and 457 A.D.).

The illustration is from a photograph taken by Dr James Burgess in 1869. Since that date the rock has been protected from further injury by a roof. The fourteen edicts of Açoka are engraved on the north-east face of the rock and cover a space of about 100 square feet. The inscription of Rudradāman occupies the top, and the inscription of Skandagupta the west face.

The edicts of Açoka have already been described (*v.* pp. 105-8). The subjoined reproduction of an impression of the second edict will serve to illustrate the beautiful Brāhmī writing of the period—the letters in the original are about two inches in height—and the translation which is appended will show the historical importance of these inscriptions.

Transliteration

(1) Savrata vijitamhi devānaṃ priyasa priyadasino rāño

(2) evam api prachaṃtesu yathā Choḍā Pāḍā Satiyaputo Keralaputo ā Taṃba-

(3) paṃṇī Aṃtiyako Yonarājā ye vāpi tasa Aṃtiyakasa sāmīpaṃ

(4) rājāno savrata devānaṃ priyasa priyadasino rāño dve chikīchhā katā

(5) manusa-chikīchhā cha pasu-chikīchhā cha osuḍhāni cha yāni manusopagāni cha

(6) paso[pa]gāni cha yata yata nāsti savrata hārāpitāni cha ropāpitāni cha

(7) mūlāni cha phalāni cha yata yata nāsti savrata hārāpitāni cha ropāpitāni cha

(8) paṃthesū kūpā cha khānāpitā vrachhā cha ropāpitā paribhogāya pasumanusānam.

Translation

'Everywhere in the realm of his Gracious Majesty, the King, the Beloved of the Gods, and likewise also in the border lands, such as (the countries of) the Cho̤las, the Pāṇḍyas, Satiyaputra, Keralaputra, as far as Ceylon, Antiochus the Greek king, or the kings in the neighbourhood of the said Antiochus, everywhere has his Gracious Majesty, the King, the Beloved of the Gods, provided remedies of two kinds, remedies for men and remedies for animals; and herbs, both such as are serviceable to men and serviceable to animals, wheresoever there were none, has he everywhere caused to be procured and planted, roots also and fruits, wheresoever there were none, has he everywhere caused to be procured and planted, and on the highways has he caused wells to be dug and trees to be planted for the enjoyment of animals and men.'

PLATE V.

A

BRĀHMĪ INSCRIPTION ON THE GIRNĀR ROCK.

[See page 150.

B

KHAROSHTHĪ INSCRIPTION ON THE BASE OF THE MATHURĀ LION-CAPITAL.

See page 158.

COINS OF ANCIENT INDIA

(Plate II, facing p. 18)

1. Punch-marked Coin

Obv. A number of symbols.

Rev. Traces of symbols. *Silver.*

This represents the primitive form of Indian coinage, which is little more than a currency of square or oblong pieces cut out of a flat plate of silver. The symbols punched on to the coin on the *obverse* are supposed to be the private marks of the money-changers, while those on the *reverse*, which are almost invariably fewer in number and of a somewhat different character, may possibly denote the locality in which the coins were issued.

2. Ancient Cast Coin

Obv. Rañò Dhamapālasa = '(Coin) of King Dharmapāla,' in very ancient Brāhmī characters written from right to left.

Rev. Blank. *Bronze.*

Coins of this class are found at the village of Eran in the Saugor District of the Central Provinces. This coin has been quoted in support of the view that the Brāhmī alphabet was originally written from right to left like Kharoshṭhī (*v.* p. 18).

3. Guild Token

Obv. Steel-yard; above, *Dujaka* or *Dojaka*, in Kharoshṭhī characters.

Rev. in incuse. *Negamā* = 'Merchants' in Brāhmī characters. *Bronze.*

The use of these tokens is uncertain, as also is the meaning of the legend on the *Obverse*.

4. Pantaleon

Obv. in incuse. Maneless lion to right; Greek legend, *Basileōs Pantaleontos* = '(Coin) of King Pantaleon.'

Rev. An Indian dancing girl; Brāhmī legend. *Rāji*[*ne*] *Paṃtalevasa.*[1] *Bronze.*

Pantaleon was one of the earliest Greek kings of Bactria to reign also in India. The square shape of this coin shows the influence of the old Indian currency of the district in which it was struck.

5. Ancient Struck Coin: Single Die

Obv. A *Chaitya*, or Buddhist shrine; to left, *Vaṭasvaka* in Brāhmī characters; to right, a standing figure worshipping; beneath him, the symbol called *nandi-pada*, 'the footprint of Nandi' (Çiva's bull).

Rev. Blank. *Bronze.*

It has been suggested that the legend *Vaṭasvaka* may denote the 'Fig-tree' (*vaṭa*) branch of the Açvakas, a people of North-Western India who may perhaps be the Assakenoi of Alexander's historians. The three early forms of Indian coinage—punch-marked, cast, and struck on one side only—are illustrated by Nos. 1, 2, and 5 respectively.

6. Sophytes

Obv. Helmeted head of king to right.

Rev. Cock to right; above, on left, a caduceus (the emblem of the Greek god Hermes); Greek legend, *Sōphutou* = '(Coin) of Sophytes.' *Silver.*

The coin is purely Greek in style. At the time of Alexander's invasion, Sophytes, whose name in its Greek form

[1] In the case of all the bilingual coins represented in this plate, the Indian legend is an exact translation of the Greek.

is supposed to represent the Sanskrit *Saubhūti*, was ruling over a kingdom in the Punjab. He entertained Alexander with the spectacle of a fight in which four of his dogs were matched against a lion. As his sporting propensities were so strong, it is possible that the cock on his coins may be a fighting cock. That sport was certainly popular in Ancient India.

7. Antialcidas

Obv. Bust of king to right; Greek legend, *Basileōs nikēphorou* | *Antialkidou* = '(Coin) of King Antialcidas, the Victorious.'

Rev. Zeus seated on a throne and holding in his right hand a figure of Nikē (the goddess of victory); on the left, the forepart of an elephant with trunk upraised; Kharoshṭhī legend, *Maharajasa jayadharasa* | *Aṃtialikitasa.* *Silver.*

The type of Zeus enthroned is frequently found on the coins of the Greek princes of the house of Eucratides to which Antialcidas belonged. For the Indian inscription in which he is mentioned, *v.* p. 134.

8. Menander

Obv. Bust of king thrusting a spear to left; Greek legend, *Basileōs sōtēros* | *Menandrou* = '(Coin) of King Menander, the Saviour.'

Rev. Athene hurling a thunder-bolt to right; Kharoshṭhī legend, *Maharajasa tratarasa* | *Menaṃdrasa.* *Silver.*

For Menander, *v.* p. 129. He belonged to the family of Euthydemus, of which the figure of Athene is the most characteristic coin-type.

9. Demetrius

Obv. Head of elephant to right.

Rev. Caduceus; Greek legend, *Basileōs Dēmētriou*, '(Coin) of King Demetrius.' *Bronze.*

10. Maues

Obv. Head of elephant to right.

Rev. Caduceus; Greek legend, *Basileōs Mauou*, '(Coin) of King Maues.' *Bronze.*

These coins, the second of which is an exact imitation of the first, show that the rule of the district in which they circulated passed from the Greeks of the house of Euthydemus to the Çakas (*v.* p. 140).

11. Eucratides

Obv. Helmeted bust of king to right.

Rev. The caps of the Dioscuri (Castor and Pollux) surmounted by stars; two palms; below, a monogram; Greek legend, *Basileōs Eukratidou* = '(Coin) of King Eucratides.' *Silver.*

12. Liaka Kusūlaka

Obv. Helmeted bust to right.

Rev. The caps of the Dioscuri; two palms; below, a monogram; Legend in Greek characters, [*Li*]*ako* [*K*]*ozoulo.* *Silver.*

Similarly these coins show the transition of the district to which they belong from the rule of the house of Eucratides to the Çakas. Liaka Kusūlaka was a satrap and the father of Pātika whose inscription at Takshaçilā was engraved in the reign of the Great King Moga (the Maues or Moa of the coins) and is dated in the seventy-eighth year of an era which has not yet been determined. (*v.* p. 141).

13. Dharaghosha, King of Audumbara

Obv. Standing figure (probably of Viçvāmitra, the rishi of the third book of the Rig-veda); Kharoshṭhī legends: (1) Around,

Mahadevasa raña Dharaghoshasa | *Oduṃbarisa* = '(Coin) of the Great Lord, King Dharaghosha | Prince of Audumbara'; (2) across, *Viçvamitra.*

Rev. Trident battle-axe; Tree within railing; Brāhmī legend (identical with the Kharoshṭhī legend (1) on the *Obverse*).

Silver.

Audambara, or the country of the Udumbaras, was situated in that region of the Punjab in which the two alphabets of Ancient India, Brāhmī and Kharoshṭhī, were used concurrently. The coins are found in the neighbourhood of Pathānkot in the Gurdāspur District. They show the influence of the Greek type of coinage. In fabric and style they somewhat resemble the coins of Apollodotus, a prince of the house of Euthydemus, and they are sometimes found in association with them. Their date would seem to be about 100 B.C.

THE BESNAGAR COLUMN

(Plate III, facing p. 134, and Plate VI, facing p. 157)

This monument is best described in the words of Dr J. H. Marshall, C.I.E., the Director General of Archæology in India. He says (*Journal of the Royal Asiatic Society*, 1909, p. 1053) :—

"When examining the ancient site of Besnagar, near Bhilsa, in the extreme south of the Gwalior State, my attention was drawn to a stone column standing near a large mound, a little to the north-east of the main site, and separated from it by a branch of the Betwa river. This column had been noticed by Sir A. Cunningham as far back as 1877, and a description of it (though not a wholly accurate one) appeared in his Report for that year. The shaft of the column is a monolith, octagonal at the base, sixteen-sided in the middle, and thirty-two-sided above, with a garland dividing the upper and middle portions; the capital is of the Persepolitan bell-shaped type, with a massive abacus surmounting it and the whole is crowned with a palm-leaf ornament of strangely unfamiliar design, which I strongly suspect did not originally belong to it. In 1877 this column was thickly encrusted from top to bottom, as it still is, with vermilion paint smeared on it by pilgrims, who generation after generation have come to worship at the spot."

The subsequent removal of the paint revealed the inscription, the historical importance of which has been already described (p. 134). A specimen of the coinage of the Græco-Indian king, Antialcidas, is shown in Plate II, No. 7 (facing p. 18). The inscription shows that the figure on the top of the column, if original, should represent Garuḍa, who has the form of a bird and is supposed to carry the god Vishṇu. There is also a smaller inscription of two lines, apparently in verse. The text and translation of the two inscriptions here given are based on

PLATE VI.

A

B

BRĀHMĪ INSCRIPTIONS ON THE BESNAGAR COLUMN.

[*See page* 137.

the readings and interpretations proposed by Dr Bloch, Dr Fleet, Prof. Barnett, and Prof. Venis, in various articles which will be found in the *Journal of the Royal Asiatic Society* for the years 1909 and 1910.

Transliteration

A

(1) Devadevasa Vā[sude]vasa Garudadhvaje ayaṃ
(2) kārite i[a] Heliodoreṇa bhāga-
(3) vatena Diyasa putreṇa Takhasilākena
(4) Yona-dūtena āgatena mahārājasa
(5) Aṃtalikitasa upa[ṃ]tā sakāsaṃ raño
(6) Kāsīput[r]asa Bhāgabhadrasa trātārasa
(7) vasena [chatu]dasemna rājena vadhamānasa

B

(1) Trini amuta-padāni — [su] anuṭhitāni
(2) nayaṃti svaga dama cāga apramāda.

Translation

A

"This Garuḍa-column of Vāsudeva (Vishṇu) the god of gods, was erected here by Heliodorus, a worshipper of Vishṇu, the son of Dion, and an inhabitant of Taxila, who came as Greek ambassador from the Great King Antialcidas to King Kāçīputra Bhāgabhadra, the Saviour, then reigning prosperously in the fourteenth year of his kingship."

B

"Three immortal precepts (footsteps) . . . when practised lead to heaven—self-restraint, charity, conscientiousness."

THE MATHURĀ LION-CAPITAL

(Plate IV, facing p. 142, and Plate V B, facing p. 150)

This capital of hard red sandstone must originally have surmounted a pillar. It was discovered by the late Pandit Bhagvānlāl Indrājī at Muttra, where it was built into the steps of an altar devoted to the worship of Çītalā, or the goddess of small-pox. The Pandit was also the first to decipher the Kharoshṭhī inscriptions with which the capital is completely covered and to recognize their great historical value (*v.* p. 142). He bequeathed the capital to the British Museum, where it may now be seen in the Gallery of Religions. The illustration facing p. 150 represents the base of the capital where it was joined to the pillar. It contains the beginning of the chief inscription. The transliteration and translation are, with a few slight changes in the former, borrowed from the edition of Dr F. W. Thomas in the *Epigraphia Indica*, vol. ix. p. 135.

Transliteration

(1) Mahachhatravasa Rajulasa
(2) agramahish(r)i-Ayasia-
(3) Komusaa dhitra
(4) Kharaostasa yuvarañã
(5) matra Nadasi-Akasa. . .

Translation

"By the Chief Queen of the Great Satrap Rājūla, daughter of Āyasi-Komūsā, mother of the Heir Apparent Kharaosta, Nandasi-Akasā (by name)" [associated with the other members of her family a relic of the Holy Sage, Buddha, was deposited in the *stūpa*].

NOTES ON THE ANCIENT GEOGRAPHY OF INDIA

(*See the map at the End*)

The names of Peoples and Countries are printed in capitals. In Ancient India they were identical, as they were in Ancient Britain in the time of Julius Cæsar. The names of Mountains and Rivers are printed in ordinary type.

Achirāvatī, *v.* Çākya.

Ākara, *v.* Mālava.

Amarāvatī, *v.* List of Cities, No. 1 (p. 172).

Andhra, the name of a tribe of Southern India inhabiting the Telugu country between the rivers Kṛishṇā (Kistna) and Godāvarī which is often called Andhra-deça, the 'Country of the Andhras.' They are mentioned in one of the later books of the Aitareya Brāhmaṇa (possibly *c.* 500 B.C.). They are described by Pliny (*Historia Naturalis*, vi. 21-23), who probably quotes from Megasthenes (*c.* 300 B.C.), as being, next to the Prasii, the most powerful of the nations of India. Their relations to the Maurya Empire are uncertain; but the manner in which they are mentioned in the inscriptions of Açoka (*c.* 250 B.C.) seems to indicate that they acknowledged its suzerainty while retaining a certain degree of independence. On the decline of the Maurya Empire their power greatly increased; and early in the second century B.C. their dominions had extended westwards across the Deccan to the District of Nāsik in the Bombay Presidency. It is probable also that at this period they came into collision with the kingdom of Magadha, now under the Çuṅgas. The dynasty under which the Andhras won this great empire bears the general name of Çātavāhana and many of its kings are called Çātakarṇi. The dynastic list is given in the Purāṇas. Its total duration is usually stated to be 456 or 460 years and the number of reigns thirty. If we suppose, therefore, that the dynasty began about 220 B.C., it would have ended about 240 A.D.; and this is probably a fairly correct statement. At various intervals during this period we are enabled from inscriptions, coins, and literature to trace the history of the Andhras with some precision. In literature they are frequently associated with their northern neighbours, the Kaliṅgas, as also in the Hāthigumphā inscription of Khāravela, the king of Kaliṅga, *c.* 150 B.C. But their most important historical monuments belong to the first half of the second century A.D. (*c.* 120-150 A.D.), the period during which they came into conflict in Western India with the Pahlava and Çaka satraps of the Kushāṇa Empire.

The decline of the Andhra Empire began about the end of the second century A.D., when the western and south-western provinces passed into the hands of another dynasty of Çātakarṇis, the Chuṭu family, to whom the designation Andhra-bhṛityas, or 'servants of the Andhras,' is specially applied. About the middle of the third century A.D., the Chuṭu family was supplanted by the Ābhīras in the west and by the Kadambas in the south-west, while the Çātavāhana family, which had continued to hold Andhra-deça in the east, was succeeded by a Rājput dynasty.

For the chief centres of Andhra rule, *v.* List of Cities—No. 1, Amarāvatī; No. 12, Pratishṭhāna; and No. 16, Vaijayantī, (pp. 172, 174, 175).

Aṅga, the Districts of Monghyr and Bhāgalpur in N. Bengal. Its capital was Champā, near the modern town of Bhāgalpur on the Ganges.

APARĀNTA, the 'Western Border,' the ancient name of the Northern Konkan, the northern portion of the strip of country lying between the Western Ghāts and the sea. Its capital was Çūrpāraka, the modern Sopāra in the Thāna District of Bombay.

ĀRYĀVARTA, the 'Land of the Aryans,' *v.* p. 50.

Asiknī, the 'Black River,' the Vedic name of the river which was afterwards called in Sanskrit the Chandrabhāgā. It is the Acesines of the historians of Alexander and the modern Chenāb. Hesychius of Alexandria, the author of a celebrated Greek lexicon (probably in the fifth century A.D.), says the name Chandrabhāgā was changed by Alexander. In its Greek form, *Sandrophagos*, it might be interpreted to mean the 'Devourer of Alexander.' He therefore preferred the older name Asiknī, the Greek form of which, Acesines, might be supposed to mean the 'Healer.'

AVANTI, *v.* MĀLAVA.

Ayodhyā, *v.* List of Cities, No. 2 (p. 172).

Bhṛigu-kaccha, *v.* List of Cities, No. 3 (p. 172).

BRAHMARSHI-DEÇA, the 'Country of the Holy Sages,' *v.* p. 50.

BRAHMĀVARTA, the 'Holy Land,' *v* p. 51.

Çākala, *v.* List of Cities, No. 4 (p. 172).

ÇĀKYA, one of the numerous Kshatriya clans living in the lowlands at the foot of the Himālayas in what is now known as the Nepalese Tarai. It is celebrated as the clan to which Buddha belonged. Its territory was bordered on the north by the mountains, on the east by the river Rohiṇī, and on the west and south by the river Achirāvatī (Rāptī). Its capital was Kapilavastu, in the neighbourhood of which was Lumbini-vana, or the 'Grove of Lumbini,' where Buddha was born (*v.* p. 67).

The Çākyas were an aristrocratic oligarchy owing some allegiance probably to the kingdom of Kosala.

Champā, *v.* Aṅga.

Chandrabhāgā, *v.* Asiknī.

Charmaṇvatī, the river Chambal, the largest tributary of the Jumna.

Chedi, the name of a people mentioned in the Rig-veda. In later times they occupied the northern portion of the Central Provinces.

Chera, *v.* Kerala.

Choḷa, a Tamil people of Southern India from whom the Coromandel Coast receives its name. (Coromandel = Sanskrit *Choḷa-maṇḍala*, the 'Province of the Choḷas'). They are mentioned in the inscriptions of Açoka (*c.* 250 B.C.) among the independent peoples living beyond the limits of the Maurya Empire. They occur also in the Mahābhārata. Other ancient literature (Tamil, Greek, and Latin) testifies to the sea-borne traffic which was carried on between the Coromandel Coast and Alexandria and thence to Europe. Evidence of the trade with Rome is afforded by the numerous Roman coins which have been discovered in various districts of Southern India. Among them has been found the gold piece which was struck by the Emperor Claudius (41-54 A.D.) to commemorate the conquest of Britain. Further evidence of the trade between Southern India and the West is supplied by words. Our *pepper* comes to us from the Tamil *pippali* through the Greek *peperi*.

Çrāvastī, *v.* List of Cities, No. 5 (p. 173).

Çūrasena, the region of Muttra in the United Provinces.

Çūrpāraka, *v.* Aparānta.

Çutudrī, the Vedic name for the Sutlej, called by the Greeks

Zadadrus or Zaradrus. Like all the great rivers of the Punjab, the Sutlej has changed its course in historical times, and some of its deserted channels are still to be traced. At present it is a tributary of the Indus; but in the time of Alexander the Great it was probably an independent river flowing into the Rann of Cutch.

Dakshiṇāpatha, the Deccan, the 'Southern Region' (Sanskrit *dakshiṇa*, Prakrit *dakkhiṇa* = 'south') as opposed to Uttarāpatha, the 'Northern Region.'

Dhānyakaṭaka, *v.* List of Cities, No. 1. Amarāvatī (p. 172).

Dṛishadvatī, the 'Stony River,' *v.* p. 51.

Gandhāra, *v.* p. 81.

Gaṅgā, the Ganges, the most celebrated of the sacred rivers of India. It is only mentioned once directly in the Rig-veda, and that in a late passage. This fact indicates that the Aryan settlers had not yet occupied the plain of the Ganges when the hymns of the Rig-veda were composed.

Girinagara, *v.* p. 149.

Girivraja, *v.* Magadha.

Godāvarī, the river of Southern India which still bears the same name.

Gomatī, the name in the Rig-veda of the present river Gumal, a tributary of the Indus.

Hastināpur, *v.* List of Cities, No. 6. Indraprastha (p. 173).

Himālaya, the 'Abode of Snow,' called in the Rig-veda Himavant, the 'Snowy Mountain,' and by the Greeks Imaus, Himaus, or Hemodus, all more or less successful attempts to reproduce in the Greek alphabet the Prakrit equivalents of the Vedic name.

Irāvatī, *v.* Parushṇī.

Kaccha, the 'Shore,' the country which still bears the same name, though it is now usually spelt Cutch. The word seems to be a Prakrit form of the Sanskrit *kaksha*, 'a girdle.'

Kāçī, the modern Benares, a small kingdom the possession of which was sometimes in dispute between its more powerful neighbours Kosala (Oudh) and Videha (Tirhut) at the period when Buddha lived. It is usually associated with Kosala.

Kaliṅga, the country lying along the east coast of India between the Mahānadī and the Godāvarī. Kaliṅga was conquered by Açoka (*v.* p. 106); but on the decline of the Maurya Empire it again became independent (*v.* p. 116).

Kāmarūpa, the ancient name of Assam.

Kāmpilya, *v.* Pañchāla.

Kapilavastu, *v.* Çākya.

Kauçāmbī, *v.* Vatsa.

Kāverī, the Cauvery River of Southern India, the 'Ganges of the South.'

Kerala, also written Chera, an ancient kingdom of Southern India comprising the modern Malabar, Cochin, and Travancore. The name of its king appears as Keralaputra in the inscriptions of Açoka.

Koṅgu-deça, the Districts of Salem and Coimbatore in the Madras Presidency.

Kosala, a kingdom lying to the east of Pañchāla and to the west of Videha. It is the modern Province of Oudh in the United Provinces. Its chief cities were Ayodhyā or Sāketa and Çrāvastī.

Kṛishṇā, the 'Black River,' the modern Kistna.

Krivi, *v.* Pañchāla.

Krumu, the name in the Rig-veda for the modern river Kurram, a western tributary of the Indus.

Kubhā, the name in the Rig-veda for the Kābul River.

Kuru, the name of the most important people of India in the time of the Brāhmaṇas. Kuru-kshetra, or the 'Field of the Kurus' (*v.* p. 47) may be described as the Eastern half of the State of Patiāla and the Delhi division of the Punjab. The holy land of Brahmāvarta lay within its border on the north-west, and its eastern limit was formed by the River Jumna. But the territories occupied by the Kurus extended to the east far beyond the limits of Kurukshetra. Their ancient capital Hastināpura was situated on the Ganges in the Meerut District of the United Provinces. They must, therefore, have occupied the northern portion of the doāb, or the region between the Jumna and the Ganges, having as their neighbours on the east the North Pañchālas, and on the south the South Pañchālas, who held the rest of the doāb as far as the land of the Vatsas, the corner where the two rivers meet at Prayāga (Allahābād). The Kurus and Pañchālas are constantly associated in early Sanskrit literature and the name Kuru-Pañchāla is often used to denote their united countries.

For the later and more celebrated capital of the Kurus, *v.* List of Cities, No. 6, Indraprastha (p. 173).

Laṅkā sometimes denotes Ceylon, and sometimes the city in the island which was the capital of the demon Rāvaṇa, whose abduction of Sītā and subsequent destruction by Rāma form part of the story of the Rāmāyaṇa.

Licchavi, *v.* Vaiçālī.

Madhya-deça, the 'Middle Country,' *v.* p. 50.

Magadha, Southern Bihār, the Districts of Gayā and Patna

in Bengal, a kingdom of the greatest political . portance in the history of Ancient and Medieval India. The rise of the Maurya Empire of Magadha is described in Chapter VII. (p. 99). Once again in later history did Magadha become the centre of a great empire, under the Gupta Dynasty, the establishment of which is marked by its era which begins in the year 319 A.D. The ancient capital of Magadha was Girivraja or Rājagṛiha, the site of which is marked by ruins at the village of Rājgīr in the Patna District. The later capital was Pāṭaliputra, for which *v.* List of Cities, No. 11 (p. 174).

Mahānadī, the 'Great River,' which still retains its name. It flows through the Orissa Division of Bengal and was the northern limit of the ancient kingdom of Kaliṅga.

Mahārāshṭra, the Marāthā Country, the Districts of Nāsik, Poona, Sātāra, and the Kolhāpur State in the Bombay Presidency. The inhabitants of this region are called Raṭhikas (Sanskrit *Rāshṭrika*) in the inscriptions of Açoka and are associated with the Pitenikas or people of Paithan.

Mālava. (1) Mālwā in Central India. It was sometimes divided into two kingdoms: Avanti or W. Mālava with its capital Ujjayinī (Ujjain), and Ākara or E. Mālava with its capital Vidiçā (Bhīlsa).

(2) (Also spelt Mālaya, or Malaya) a people living in the Punjab and known from Sanskrit literature. They are the Malli of the historians of Alexander the Great.

The name was probably that of a tribe which had settlements in different parts of India.

Maru, the Thar or Great Indian Desert of Rājputāna.

Mathurā, *v.* List of Cities, No. 9 (p. 174).

Matsya, the name of a people mentioned in the Rig-veda. In the period of the Mahābhārata they lived to the south of the

Kurus and to the west of the Çūrasenas. Their country is the modern State of Alwar in Rājputāna and some adjacent districts.

Mithilā, *v.* List of Cities, No. 10 (p. 174)

Narmadā, the modern river Narbadā.

Nishadha, an ancient kingdom on the south of the Vindhya Mountains. It lay to the south of Mālava and to the north-west of Vidarbha. It is best known as the realm of King Nala, in the 'Story of Nala,' an episode of the Mahābhārata.

Pallava, a people of Southern India having as their capital Kāñchī (Conjeeveram).

Pañchāla, a people who appear to be identical with the Krivis mentioned in the Rig-veda. The name would suggest that they were a confederation of five tribes (Sanskrit *pañcha*, 'five'). In history they are sometimes divided into two kingdoms—South Pañchāla, the country between the Jumna and Ganges to the east and south-east of the Kurus and Çūrasenas, and North Pañchāla, districts of the United Provinces lying east of the Ganges and north-west of the Province of Oudh. The capital of South Pañchala was Kāmpilya, now represented by ruins at the village of Kāmpil in the Farrukhābād District. It appears in the Mahābhārata as the capital of King Drupada, the father of Kṛishṇā or Draupadī, who became the wife of the five sons of Pāṇḍu. The capital of North Pañchāla was Ahicchatra, also mentioned in the Mahābhārata and now a ruined site still bearing the same name near the village of Rāmnagar in the Bareilly District.

The Pañchālas are often associated with the Kurus: *v.* Kuru.

Pāṇḍya, an ancient people occupying the modern Districts of Madura and Tinnevelly in the extreme south of India. They are mentioned by Greek and Latin authors and also by the Emperor Açoka in his edicts.

Paropanisus, sometimes written Paropamisus, the Greek name for the Hindu Kush which was also sometimes called the Indian Caucasus. It is the Greek form of *Paruparesanna*, the name which the people of this region bear in the Babylonian and Susian versions of the inscription of Darius at Behistun (*v.* p. 84).

Parushṇī, the name in the Rig-veda of the river which is called in later Sanskrit Irāvatī, the modern Rāvi. It is the Hydraotes of the Greeks. It is celebrated in the Rig-veda in connexion with the victory of Sudās over the ten kings.

Pāṭaliputra, *v.* List of Cities, No. 11 (p. 174).

Pratishṭhāna, *v.* List of Cities, No. 12 (p. 174).

Prayāga, *v.* List of Cities, No. 13 (p. 175).

Rājagṛiha, *v.* Magadha.

Rohiṇī, *v.* Çākya.

Sadānīra, *v.* Videha.

Samataṭa, the 'Even Shore,' the ancient name of the Ganges delta.

Sarasvatī, the 'River of Lakes,' *v.* p. 51.

Sindhu, the ancient name of the Indus, the river from which India derives its name (*v.* p. 24).

Sindhu-Sauvīra, the lower valley of the Indus, approximately the modern Province of Sind. The two parts of the compound are often used separately as names having much the same meaning.

Siprā, *v.* List of Cities, No. 15. Ujjayinī (p. 175).

Surāshṭra, the 'Good Kingdom,' Kāthiāwār and a part of

Gujarāt in Western India. The name survives in the modern name Surat.

Suvāstu, the 'River of Good Dwellings,' the name in the Rig-veda for the Swāt, a tributary of the Kābul River.

Takshaçilā, *v.* List of Cities, No. 14 (p. 175).

Tāmraparṇī. (1) the Sanskrit name of a town in Ceylon, sometimes used in a wider sense to denote the whole island. In this latter sense it occurs in its Pali form *Tambapaṇṇi* in Buddhist literature and in the inscriptions of Açoka. It is known to Greek and Latin writers as Taprobane. (2) Tāmbraparni, a river in the Tinnevelly Dist. of Madras.

Tāpī, the Sanskrit name of the modern river Tāpti in Western India.

Ujjayinī, *v.* List of Cities, No. 15 (p. 175).

Vaiçālī, the modern Basārh in the Hājīpur subdivision which occupies the south-western corner of the Muzaffarpur District of Bengal. The ancient site is marked by a large mound of ruins and by a magnificent uninscribed pillar of Açoka which is surmounted by the figure of a lion. It is described by the Chinese Buddhist pilgrim, Hiuen Tsiang, who visited the spot early in the seventh century A.D. In the sixth century B.C. Vaiçālī was the seat of a small but powerful aristocratic oligarchy of nobles belonging to the Licchavi clan which seems to have been a branch of the Vṛiji tribe. The Vṛijis formed a confederacy, and the country of the Vṛijis seems to have included not only Vaiçālī but also the larger adjoining realm of Videha. It was at Kuṇḍapura, the modern Basukund, a suburb of Vaiçālī, that Vardhamāna Jñātaputra, the founder of Jainism, was born. Vaiçālī was famous also in the annals of Buddhism; and it was here that the Second Buddhist Council was held a hundred years after Buddha's death for the purpose of correcting certain abuses which had grown up in the doctrine and practices of the religious community. Vaiçālī, situated near the opposite bank of the Ganges, was a standing menace to Pāṭaliputra and stood in the way of the expansion of the kingdom of Magadha. It was accordingly reduced to submission by Ajātaçatru, the king of Magadha, shortly after Buddha's death. The removal of this obstacle cleared the way for the extension of the political influence of Magadha not only over Videha (Tirhut) but also over Kosala (Oudh), and is therefore an important fact in the growth of the empire of Magadha.

Vaijayantī, *v.* List of Cities, No. 16 (p. 175).

VAṄGA, the old form of the modern name Bengal. It denoted the western and central districts of the present province, *viz.* Murshidābād, Bīrbhūm, Burdwān, and Nadiā.

VATSA, the region of Prayāga (*v.* List of Cities, No. 13), or Allahābād in the United Provinces. Its capital was Kauçāmbī which has been identified, though not with absolute certainty, with Kosam, the name borne by two adjacent villages (Kosam Inam and Kosam Khirāj) in the Allahābād District.

VIDARBHA, the modern Berār, now attached to the Central Provinces. It was the kingdom of Bhīma, the father of Damayantī, the heroine of the 'Story of Nala.' The tradition of a war between Magadha and Vidarbha is preserved in Kālidāsa's historical drama *Mālavikāgnimitra* (*c.* 400 A.D). Kālidāsa, like Shakespeare, was probably careless about details of ancient history or geography; and some of the information which we derive from the *Mālavikāgnimitra* is no doubt inexact. If we may correct and supplement this information from other sources, we may suppose that early in the second century B.C., when the Çuṅga king Pushyamitra was reigning over Magadha with his son Agnimitra as viceroy of the Province of Mālava, there was a war between Mālava and Vidarbha, which was at that period probably a province of the Andhra Empire.

Videha, Tirhut or Northern Bihār. It probably comprised the districts of Champāran, Muzaffarpur, and Darbhangā in the Province of Bengal. In its south-west corner (the Hājīpur subdivision of the Muzaffarpur District) lay the little state of Vaiçālī. Videha was separated from Magadha (S. Bihār) by the Ganges, and from Kosala (Oudh) by the river Sadānīra, probably the Great Gandak. It was the realm of King Janaka, the father of Sītā, the heroine of the Rāmāyaṇa. Its capital was Mithilā.

Vidiçā, *v.* Mālava.

Vipāç or Vipāçā, the Hyphasis of the Greeks and the modern Beās.

Vindhya, the range of mountains still bearing the same name. It is usually regarded in Sanskrit literature as the natural boundary between Northern and Southern India.

Vitastā, the name in the Rig-veda for the Hydaspes of Alexander's historians and the modern river Jhelum. Latin classical writers use 'Hydaspes,' like 'Britain,' to denote some far remote region on the confines of the habitable world; *e.g.* Horace (*Odes* I. xxii):

quæ loca fabulosus
Lambit Hydaspes.

These geographical references are not always strictly correct, as, for example, Virgil's 'Medus Hydaspes' (*Georgics*, iv. 211) which would place the river in Persia.

Vṛiji, *v.* Vaiçālī.

Yamunā, the 'Twin River,' the Jumna, the sister of the Ganges. It is mentioned three times in the Rig-veda. At that period it probably marked the extreme limit to which the Aryan settlements had yet extended.

LIST OF CITIES INDICATED BY NUMERALS IN THE MAP (AT THE END)

1. Amarāvatī, 'the Abode of the Immortals,' a village in the Guntūr District of Madras on the Kṛishṇā (Kistna) River. Near it stood Dhānyakaṭaka (Dhāranikotta) one of the capitals of Andhra-deça, 'the Country of the Andhras.' Amarāvatī is famous for its Buddhist *stūpa*, once probably the most magnificent of all the monuments of India, but now ruined by the vandalism of modern times. Some of its sculptures in white marble are preserved on the great staircase of the British Museum and others in the Madras Museum.

2. Ayodhyā, the modern Ajodhyā, a sacred town on the Gogrā River in the Fyzābād District of the United Provinces. It was the capital of the kingdom of Kosala (Oudh), and the residence of King Daçaratha, the father of Rāma the hero of the Rāmāyaṇa. Oudh (Awadh) is simply the modern form of the name.

In Buddhist literature Sāketa appears as the capital of Kosala, and as one of the largest cities of India. It has been supposed that either Sāketa and Ayodhyā were identical or that they were adjacent cities like London and Westminster.

3. Bhṛigu-kaccha, 'the Shore of Bhṛigu' a legendary king, later spelt Bhāru-kaccha, the Greek Barugaza and the modern Broach, a town in the Bombay Presidency near the mouth of the Narmadā (Narbadā). In ancient times it was a famous sea-port.

4. Çākala, the modern Siālkot in the Lahore Division of the Punjab, was the capital of the Madras who are known in the later Vedic period (Bṛihadāraṇyaka Upanishad). Çākala-dvīpa, or the 'island' of Çākala, was the name for the *doāb*, or land lying between the two rivers Chandrabhāgā (Chenāb) and Irāvatī (Rāvi). Çākala was the capital, or one of the capitals,

of the Greek kings of the House of Euthydemus, and the residence of Menander (Milinda) (*v.* p. 130). After the invasion of the Hūṇas (Huns) in the last quarter of the fifth century A.D., it became the capital of Toramāṇa and his son Mihirakula.

5. Çrāvastī, the modern Set Mahet in the Gondā District of Oudh, a city of the kingdom of Kosala intimately associated with the teaching of Buddha. Many of his discourses are said to have been delivered while he was residing there in the monastery of the Jetavana, a large park which had been purchased for him from Prince Jeta by the wealthy merchant Anāthapiṇḍika. The price was represented by the number of the square coins of the period (*v.* Plate II. 1), which when placed edge to edge sufficed to cover the ground. This purchase is the subject of a bas-relief on the great Buddhist *stūpa* at Bhārhut, in the Nāgod State of Central India.

6. Indraprastha, the modern Indarpat near Delhi, was the second capital of the Kurus. According to the story told in the Mahābhārata, the blind king, Dhṛitarāshṭra, with his hundred sons, continued to rule at the old capital Hastināpura on the Ganges, while he assigned to his nephews, the five Pāṇḍus, a district on the Jumna where they founded Indraprastha. The 'Field of the Kurus,' or the region of Delhi, was the scene of the subsequent war between the Kurus and the Pāṇḍus when, according to the epic in its present form, all the nations of India were ranged on one side or the other; and it has been the great battlefield of India ever since, as it forms a narrow strip of habitable country lying between the Himālayas and the Indian Desert through which every invading army from the Punjab must force its way. Because of this strategical importance Delhi became the capital of India under the Mughal emperors, who came into India by land from the north-west. The British, on the other hand, who came by sea made their earliest capitals near the coast.

7. Kāñchī, the modern Conjeeveram (*Kāchī -puram*) in the Chingleput District of Madras. It was the capital of the Pallavas.

8. Kānyakubja, the modern Kanauj in the Farrukhābā District of the United Provinces, an ancient city famous in Indian history. The fanciful derivation of its name from the two Sanskrit words, *kanyā* 'a maiden' and *kubja* 'hunchback,' gave rise to the legend, told in the first book of the Rāmāyaṇa, of the hundred daughters of King Kuçanābha who were condemned to this deformity by the curse of the rishi Vāyu as a punishment for declining his offer of marriage. The story is also told, with variations, by the Chinese Buddhist pilgrim, Hiuen Tsiang, who visited the court of King Harshavardhana at Kanauj early in the seventh century A.D.

9. Mathurā, which still retains its ancient name now usually written Muttra, is a city in the Agra Division of the United Provinces. It was the capital of the Çūrasenas, and, as being the birthplace of the god Kṛishṇa, it was held sacred by the Hindus. It was governed by native princes, whose names are known from their coins, in the second century B.C., and it passed from them into the possession of one of the families of Çaka satraps, *c.* 100 B.C. (*v.* the Lion Capital of Mathurā on Plate IV, and the note on p. 158). Under the Kushāṇa Empire it was an important religious centre of the Jains.

10. Mithilā, the capital of the kingdom of Videha (Tirhut or N. Bihār) and the residence of King Janaka, the father of Sītā the heroine of the Rāmāyaṇa.

11. Pāṭaliputra, the modern Patna, the capital of Magadha under the Maurya Empire. It is described by Megasthenes, the Greek ambassador of Seleucus, king of Syria, who visited the court of Chandragupta, *c.* 300 B.C. (*v.* p. 102).

12. Pratishṭhāna, the modern Paithan on the Godāvarī in

the Aurangābād District of the Nizām's Dominions. It was the capital of the western provinces of the Andhra Empire.

13. Prayāga, the modern Allahābād in the United Provinces. It is the sacred region where Ganges and Jumna meet.

14. Takshaçilā, the Taxila of the Greeks. Its site is marked by miles of ruins near Shāhdheri or Dher i Shāhan, the 'Mound of the Kings,' in the Rāwalpindi District of the Punjab. It was the most celebrated University town of Ancient India where students learnt 'the three Vedas (Rig, Yajur, and Sāman) and the eighteen arts.' The district of Takshaçilā sometimes formed an independent kingdom, as in the days of Alexander the Great; but it is often regarded as a province of the kingdom of Gandhāra.

15. Ujjayinī on the Siprā, a tributary of the Charmaṇvatī (Chambal), is the modern Ujjain in Gwalior, Central India. It was the capital of Avanti or W. Mālava, and the residence of the viceroy of the western provinces both under the Maurya and the Gupta Empires. Owing to its position it became a great commercial centre. Here met the three routes, from the Western Coast with its sea-ports Çūrpāraka (Sopāra) and Bhṛigukaccha (Broach), from the Deccan, and from Çrāvastī in Kosala (Oudh). It was also a great centre of science and literature. The Hindu astronomers reckoned their first meridian of longitude from Ujjayinī, and the dramas of Kālidāsa were performed on the occasion of the Spring Festival before its viceregal court, c. 400 A.D.

16. Vaijayantī, the modern Banavāsi in the N. Kanara District of the Bombay Presidency. It was the capital of the south-western provinces of the Andhra Empire. It was afterwards held by the Chuṭu family of Çātakarṇis and from them it passed to the Kadambas.

SHORT BIBLIOGRAPHY

GENERAL SURVEYS

The Imperial Gazetteer of India (new edition): The Indian Empire, Vol. II. Historical. Oxford, 1908.

Pp. 1-88. Fleet, J. F., *Epigraphy.*

Pp. 101-134. Smith, V. A., *Archæology of the Historical Period.*

Pp. 135-154. Smith, V. A., *Numismatics.*

Pp. 155-205. Burgess, J., *Architecture.*

Pp. 206-269. Macdonell, A. A., *Sanskrit Literature.*

Pp. 270-302. Smith, V. A., *Early History of Northern India.*

Gazetteer of the Bombay Presidency.

I. i. Bombay, 1896.

Pp. 1-147. Bhagvānlāl Indrājī, *Early History of Gujarāt.*

I. ii. Bombay, 1896.

Pp. 132-275. Bhandārkar, R. G., *History of the Dekkan.*

(Second edition. Bombay, 1895.)

Pp. 277-584. Fleet, J. F., *Dynasties of the Kanarese Districts.*

Grundriss der indo-arischen Philologie und Altertumskunde Strassburg.

I. 11. Bühler, G., *Indische Paläographie,* 1896.

II. 1a. Bloomfield, M., *The Atharvaveda and the Gopatha-Brāhmaṇa*, 1899.

II. 3b. Rapson, E. J., *Indian Coins*, 1897.

Grundriss der iranischen Philologie. Strassburg. II. Band. Litteratur, Geschichte und Kultur, 1896-1904.

Pp. 54-74. Weissbach, F. H., *Die altpersischen Inschriften*.

Pp. 371-394. Geiger, W., *Geographie von Iran*.

Pp. 395-550. Justi, F., *Geschichte Irans von den ältesten Zeiten bis zum Ausgang der Sāsāniden*.

THE LITERATURES OF ANCIENT INDIA

Hopkins, E. W., *The Great Epic of India*. New York, 1901.

Kaegi, A., *The Rigveda*. (English trans. by Arrowsmith.) Boston, 1886.

Macdonell, A. A., *A History of Sanskrit Literature*. London, 1900.

von Schroeder, L., *Indiens Literatur und Cultur*. Leipzig, 1887.

Winternitz, M., Geschichte der indischen Litteratur. Leipzig. I. Band. *Einleitung—Der Veda—Die volkstümlichen Epen und die Purāṇas*. (Zweite Ausgabe.) 1909.
II. Band, Erste Hälfte. *Die Buddhistische Litteratur*. 1913.

HISTORY, GEOGRAPHY, AND ANTIQUITIES

(Bactria)

Gardner, P., *The Coins of the Greek and Scythic Kings of Bactria and India*. (British Museum Catalogue.) London, 1886.

Rawlinson, H. G., *Bactria*. London, 1912.

(PERSIA, SYRIA, AND PARTHIA)

Babelon, E., *Les Perses Achéménides.* Paris, 1893.

———, *Les Rois de Syrie.* Paris, 1890.

Bevan, E. R., *The House of Seleucus.* London, 1902.

von Gutschmid, A., *Geschichte Irans.* Tübingen, 1888.

King, L. W., & Thompson, R. C., *The Sculptures and Inscriptions of Darius the Great on the Rock of Behistun in Persia.* London, 1907.

Rawlinson, G., *The five great Monarchies of the ancient Eastern World.* Fourth Edition, Vol. III. London, 1879.

———, *The sixth great Oriental Monarchy.* London, 1873.

Wroth, W. W., *Catalogue of the Coins of Parthia.* (British Museum Catalogue.) London, 1903.

(INDIA)

Barnett, L. D., *Antiquities of India.* London, 1913.

Bühler, J. G., & Burgess, J., *The Indian Sect of the Jainas.* London, 1903.

Cunningham, A., *Coins of Ancient India.* London, 1891.

———, *Coins of Alexander's Successors in the East.* (Reprinted from the *Numismatic Chronicle*, 1868-1873.) London, 1873.

———, *Coins of the Indo-Scythians.* (Reprinted from the *Numismatic Chronicle*, 1888-1892.) London, 1892.

———, *Coins of the Later Indo-Scythians.* (Reprinted from the *Numismatic Chronicle*, 1893-4.) London, 1894.

———, *The Ancient Geography of India.* London, 1871.

Davids, T. W. Rhys, *Ancient Coins and Measures of Ceylon* London, 1877.

———, *Buddhist India.* London, 1903.

Duff, Miss C. M. (Rickmers, Mrs W. R.), *The Chronology of India from the earliest times to the beginning of the sixteenth century.* Westminster, 1899.

Elliot, W., *Coins of Southern India.* London, 1886.

Foucher, A., *Notes sur la Géographie ancienne du Gandhara.* (Reprinted from the *Bulletin de l'École Française d'Extrême Orient.*) Hanoi, 1892.

Geiger, W., *The Mahāvaṃsa, or the Great Chronicle of Ceylon.* Oxford, 1912.

Joppen, C., *Historical Atlas of India.* Third edition. London, 1914.

Lüders, H., *A List of Brāhmī Inscriptions from the earliest times to about* A.D. 400. (Appendix to Vol. x. of the *Epigraphia Indica.*) Calcutta, 1910.

Macdonell, A. A., and Keith, A. B., *Vedic Index of Names and Subjects.* London, 1912.

Pargiter, F. E., *The Mārkaṇḍeya Purāṇa.* (Translated into English with geographical notes.) Calcutta, 1904.

Rapson, E. J., *Catalogue of the Coins of the Andhra Dynasty, etc.* (British Museum Catalogue.) London, 1908.

Senart, E., *Les Inscriptions de Piyadasi.* Paris, 1881-6.

Smith, V. A., *The Early History of India.* Third edition. Oxford, 1914.

———, *Asoka.* Second edition. Oxford, 1909.

Zimmer, H., *Altindisches Leben*, Berlin, 1879.

(India as described by Greek and Latin Writers)

Holdich, T., *The Gates of India.* London, 1910.

M'Crindle, J. W., *Ancient India as described by Megasthenes and Arrian.* (Reprinted from the *Indian Antiquary.*) Calcutta, 1877.

———, *The Commerce and Navigation of the Erythræan Sea.* (Reprinted from the *Indian Antiquary.*) Calcutta, 1879.

———, *Ancient India as described by Ktêsias the Knidian.* (Reprinted from the *Indian Antiquary*, 1881.) Calcutta, 1882.

M'Crindle, J. W., *Ancient India as describea by Ptolemy.* (Reprinted from the *Indian Antiquary*, 1884.) Calcutta, 1885.

———, *The Invasion of India by Alexander the Great.* Second edition. Westminster, 1896.

———, *Ancient India as described in Classical Literature.* Westminster, 1901.

Schoff, W. H., *The Periplus of the Erythræan Sea.* (Translated and Annotated.) London, 1912.

OUTLINES OF CHRONOLOGY

It must be understood that many of the dates given are only approximately correct.

B.C.

1200–1000. Earliest Vedic hymns.

1000–800. Period of the Vedic collections—Rig-veda, Sāma-veda, Yajur-veda, and Atharva-veda.

800–600. Period of the Brāhmaṇas.

600. The earliest Upanishads.

660–583. Zoroaster, the founder of the religion of the Avesta.

600–200. Period of the Sūtras.

599–527. Vardhamāna Jñātaputra, the founder of Jainism.

563–483. Siddhārtha Gautama, the founder of Buddhism:

558–530. Cyrus, king of Persia.
The conquest of Gandhāra took place in his reign.

543–491. Bimbisāra, king of Magadha, contemporary with Buddha.

522–486. Darius I, king of Persia.
The expedition of Scylax and the conquest of 'India,' = the country of the Indus, took place in his reign, *c.* 510 B.C.

491–459. Ajātaçatru, king of Magadha, contemporary with Buddha.

400–300. Period of the Mahābhārata.

400–200. Period of the Rāmāyaṇa.

B.C.

343–321. The Nanda dynasty of Magadha.

336–323. Alexander the Great, king of Macedon.

331. The battle of Gaugamela.

The Persian empire and, in theory, its Indian provinces come under the sway of Alexander the Great.

327–325. Indian expedition of Alexander the Great.

321–184. The Maurya dynasty of Magadha.

321–297. Chandragupta, king of Magadha, founder of the Maurya empire.

312–280. Seleucus Nicator, king of Syria.

The Seleucid era dates from the beginning of his reign.

305. Invasion of the Punjab by Seleucus Nicator.

297–269. Bindusāra, king of Magadha and Maurya emperor.

285–258. Magas, king of Cyrene, contemporary with Açoka.

285–247. Ptolemy Philadelphus, king of Egypt, contemporary with Açoka.

277–239. Antigonus Gonatas, king of Macedon, contemporary with Açoka.

272. Accession of Alexander, king of Epirus, contemporary with Açoka.

269–227. Açoka, king of Magadha and Maurya emperor.

The dates in Açoka's inscription are reckoned from his coronation in 264 B.C.

261–246. Antiochus II Theos, king of Syria, contemporary with Açoka.

256. Conquest of Kaliṅga by Açoka in the ninth year after his coronation.

250. Establishment of the kingdom of Bactria by Diodotus, and of the kingdom of Parthia by Arsaces.

247–207. Tissa, king of Ceylon, contemporary with Açoka.

B.C.

246. Introduction of Buddhism into Ceylon by Mahendra (Mahinda).

230. Euthydemus, king of Bactria, supplants the house of Diodotus.

220. Establishment of the Andhra power (Çātavāhana dynasty).

209. Invasion of Bactria and the Kābul Valley by Antiochus III the Great, king of Syria (223-187 B.C.).

200–100. Græco-Indian kings of the house of Euthydemus ruling in N.W. India.

The Indian conquests of the Græco-Bactrian kings began in the reign of Euthydemus (*c.* 200 B.C.). They were extended over the Kābul Valley, Gandhāra, and 'India' = the country of the Indus, by Demetrius (*c.* 195 B.C.). This house was deprived of its possessions in Bactria, in the Kābul Valley, and in Gandhāra by Eucratides (*c.* 175 B.C.) Subsequently, the chief centre of its power lay in the E. Punjab. The chief princes of this house after Demetrius were Apollodotus, Menander, and the Stratos.

184–72. The Çuṅga dynasty of Magadha and Mālava.

The first king, Pushyamitra, ruled over Magadha, with his son, Agnimitra, as viceroy of Mālava. It is possible that the king Bhāgabhadra, who had political relations with Antialcidas, a Græco-Indian king of the house of Eucratides, may have been the Çuṅga viceroy of Mālava (p. 134).

175–25. Græco-Indian kings of the house of Eucratides ruling in N.W. India.

Eucratides wrested the Kābul Valley and Gandhāra from the house of Euthydemus; and kings of

B.C.

his house held these provinces together with possessions in Bactria until the Çaka invasion of Bactria (*c.* 135 B.C.), after which their rule was confined to territories south of the Hindu Kush. They were deprived of Gandhāra by the Çakas *c.* 100 B.C., and of the Kābul Valley by the Kushāṇas *c.* 25 B.C. The immediate successors of Eucratides were Heliocles and Antialcidas. The last king of this house was Hermæus.

171–138. Mithradates I., king of Parthia.

He invaded Bactria in the reign of Eucratides.

150. Khāravela, king of Kaliṅga.

135. The Çaka invasion of Bactria.

100. The Çaka invasion of N.W. India.

The Çakas conquered the Punjab from the Græco-Indian kings of the house of Euthydemus and Gandhāra from the Græco-Indian kings of the house of Eucratides.

58. Initial year of the Vikrama era.

The establishment of this era marks the defeat of the Çakas in Mālava by a king who is known as Vikramāditya.

50. A Pahlava dynasty (the family of Vonones) ruling in N.W. India.

The precise relations of the Pahlavas (the family of Vonones) to the Çakas (the family of Maues) are uncertain; but there was undoubtedly some connexion between them. It is probable that the two peoples had been associated for centuries in the eastern provinces (Drangiāna = Seistān and Arachosia = Kandahār) of the Persian and Parthian empires. The appearance of the family of Vonones in India seems to denote the extension to India of

B.C.

a Parthian power already established in these eastern provinces.

25. Conquest of the Kābul Valley by the Kushāṇa chief Kujūla Kadphises.

The evidence of coins seems to indicate that Kujūla Kadphises was contemporary with the Roman emperor Augustus (27 B.C.-14 A.D.). His conquest of the last remaining Græco-Indian kingdom in the Kābul Valley marks the beginning of the extension of the Kushāṇa power from Bactria to India. During the period of his rule in the Kābul Valley, Gandhāra, the Punjab, and Sind were still held by the Pahlavas and the Çakas.

A.D.

21–50. Gondopharnes, Pahlava king of N.W. India.

The Pahlava power culminated and probably began to decline under this king. His Takht-i-Bhai inscription shows that he ruled in Gandhāra, and, if its dates are correctly interpreted, that he began to reign in 21 A.D. and was still reigning in 47 A.D.

30. Wima Kadphises, Kushāṇa king.

The extension of the Kushāṇa power from the Kābul Valley to 'India' = the country of the Indus, began in his reign.

78. Kanishka, Kushāṇa king.

The Çaka era, so called at a later date because it was used for more than three centuries by the Çaka kings of Surāshṭra, originally satraps of the Kushāṇas, probably marks the establishment of the Kushāṇa empire under Kanishka.

See "Notes on the Ancient Geography of India," pages 159-175.

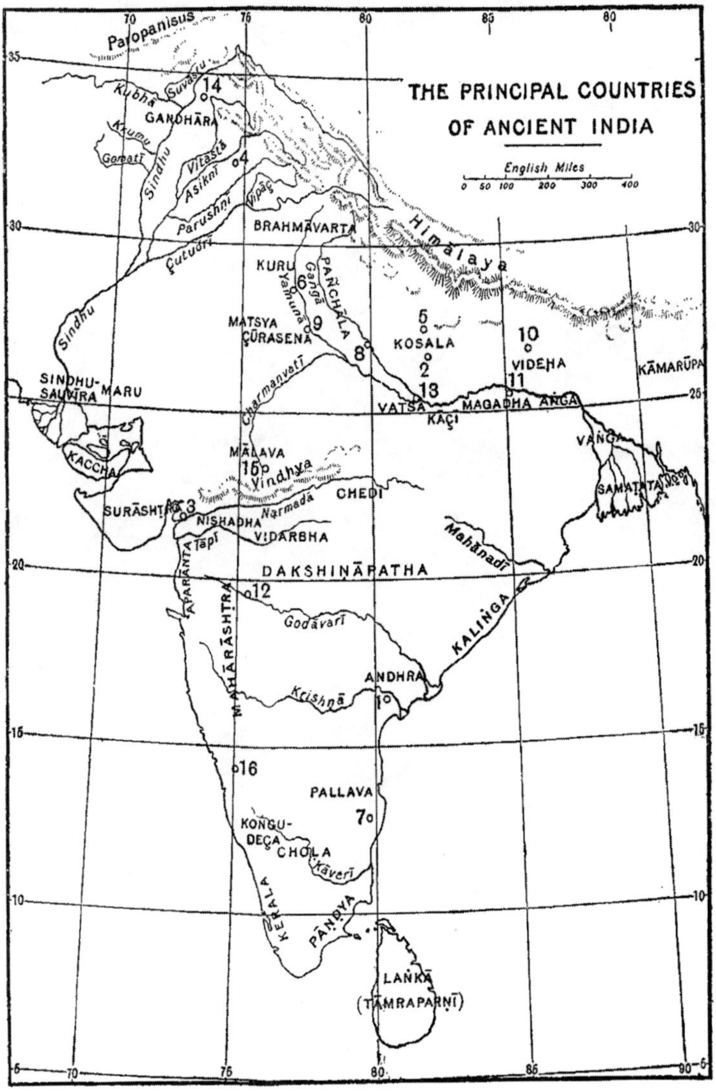

LIST OF CITIES INDICATED BY NUMERALS. [*See pages* 172-175.

1. Amarāvatī.
2. Ayodhyā.
3. Bhṛigu-kaccha.
4. Çākala.
5. Çrāvastī.
6. Indraprastha.
7. Kāñchī.
8. Kānyakubja.
9. Mathurā.
10. Mithilā.
11. Pāṭaliputra.
12. Pratishṭhāna.
13. Prayāga.
14. Takshaçilā.
15. Ujjayinī.
16. Vaijayantī.

INDEX

Important references are separated from the rest by a semicolon

Ābhīra, 160
Acesines = Chandrabhāgā = Chenāb = Asiknī, *q.v.*
Achirāvatī = Rāptī, 161
Açoka, Maurya emperor, 104-109; 118
contemporary Hellenic sovereigns mentioned in his edicts, 21
sent missionaries to Hellenic kingdoms, 108
erected a pillar to mark Buddha's birthplace, 67, 106
conquest of Kaliṅga, 116
extent of his dominions, 20, 107
religious toleration in his reign, 112
his heir-apparent mentioned in his edicts, 109
his grandson Daçaratha, 110
Girnār inscription, 149
v. also inscriptions as sources of history
āçrama, 59
Acts of St Thomas, 145
Açvaka, 152
Açvins, 80
Adhvaryu, 46
Agni = Lat. *ignis*, 42
Agnimitra, Çuṅga king, Viceroy of Mālava, 114, 170
Ahicchatra, capital of N. Pañchāla, 167
Airya = Aryan, 5
Aitareya Brāhmaṇa, 54, 159
Ajātaçatru (1) king of Kāçī, 62
(2) king of Magadha, 170
Ājīvikas, Jain ascetics, 110
Akbar, Mughal emperor, 103
Alexander the Great, king of Macedon:
invasion of the Punjab, 88-96; 24, 120
historians, 89, 90; 20, 127
continued the Persian system of government by satraps, 95-6; 141
no traces of his invasion left in Indian literature or institutions, 97, 134
division of the Macedonian empire after his death, 101
Alexander, king of Epirus, 21
Alexandria-sub-Caucasum, 89
alphabets, ancient, their decipherment, 18, 19, 82, 126
v. also Cuneiform, Brāhmī, Kharoshṭhī, Greek
Amarāvatī, 172
Amitrochates = Skt. *Amitraghāta*, a title of Bindusāra, 103
Anabasis of Alexander, 90, 94
Anāthapiṇḍika, 173
Andhra, people and kingdom, 116-7, 159-60
Andhra-bhṛitya family of Andhra kings, 160
Aṅga, 160
Antialcidas, Græco-Indian king of the house of Eucratides, 134, 157
coin of, 153

Antigonus Gonatas, king of Macedon, 21
Antiochus I Soter, king of Syria, 103
Antiochus II Theos, king of Syria, 21, 107, 118, 150
Antiochus III the Great, king of Syria:
  his invasion of the Kābul Valley, 119-21
Aornos, 91-2
Aparānta, 161
Apollodotus, Græco-Indian king of the house of Euthydemus, 128, 130, 133, 141, 155
Arachosia = Kandahār, 88, 138, 140, 144
Āraṇyakas, 58-9
arhat, 57
Aria, 88
Arrian, 90, 94
Arsaces, first king of Parthia, 118
Artabanus I, king of Parthia, 119
Artabanus II, king of Parthia, 137
Artaxerxes II Mnemon, king of Persia, 83
Artha-çāstra, 103
arthavāda, 53
Ārya = Aryan, 5
Aryan group of Indo-European family:
  Persians and Indians, 29-31, 43
  migration into India, 31, 40; 26
  progress of civilization, 31-33
  civilization depicted in—
    Rig-veda, 40-46
    Yajur-veda, 46-49
    Atharva-veda, 49, 50
  languages, 29-31
  kings of Mitanni with Aryan names, 80
  non-Brahmanical Aryans, 55
Āryāvarta, 50
Asiknī = Chandrabhāga = Acesines = Chenāb, 161; 92
Assakenoi, 152
Assam = Kāmarūpa, 164
Assyria, 79
astronomy, Hindu and Greek, 132
Atharva-veda, 49, 50; 81
Athene, figure of, *v.* coin-types
ātman, 59, 61
Audambara, coin of, 154-5
Augustus, Roman emperor, 122
Aurōra, 43
Avanti = W. Mālava, 166, 175
Avesta, 30; 4, 24
Āyasi-Komūsā, 158
Ayodhyā, 172; 115
Azes, Çaka king, 144

BABYLON, Babylonia, 79, 80, 101
Babylonian language, 82, 84, 168
Bactria = Balkh, occupied by Persian Aryans, 30
  conquered by Alexander the Great, 89
  Hellenic kingdom, 118-120, 124; 122-3, 134
  its coins, 120, 125
  transference of Greek rule to India, 125
  Parthian invasion, 126
  Çaka invasion, 127; 125, 137
  Yueh-chi occupation, 127, 128
Baluchistān, *v.* Gedrosia
Barnett, Prof. L. D., 157
Barugaza = Broach = Bhṛigu-kaccha, *q.v.*
Beās = Hyphasis = Vipāç or Vipāçā, *q.v.*
Behistun, inscriptions of Darius at, 82, 84, 168
Benares = Kāçī, 164
Bengal = Vaṅga, 170
Bengal, Asiatic Society of, 6
Besnagar: column, 156
  inscription, 134, 157
Bhadra or Bhadraka, Çuṅga king, 134
Bhāgabhadra, Kāçīputra, king reigning at Besnagar, 134, 157
Bhagvānlāl Indrājī, Pandit, 142, 158

Bharata, 25
Bhārata or Bhārata-varsha, 25
Bhārhut *stūpa*, 115, 173
Bhīma, king of Vidarbha, 170
Bhṛigu-kaccha or Bhāru-kaccha = Barugaza = Broach, 129, 130, 172, 175
bilingual coins, 18-9, 125-6, 152-5
Bindusāra, Maurya emperor, 103
Bloch, Dr, 157
Bolān Pass, 140
Bopp, Franz, 2
Brahman (Brāhmaṇa) caste, 45, 59
  its literature, 8, 11
Brāhmaṇas, 53-9; 76
  language, 11, 55-6
  geography, 56
  religion, 57-8
Brahmanism, 34, 55, 68
  sacred language of, 14, 69
Brahmarshi-deça, 50-1
Brahmāvarta, 51
Brāhmī alphabet, 17-8, 149-50
  coin-legends, 151-2, 155
  inscriptions, 150, 157
Brāhūī language, 29
Bṛihadāraṇyaka Upanishad, 172
Bṛihadratha, Maurya king, 114
British dominion in India, 26, 34
Broach = Bhṛigu-kaccha, *q.v.*
Bucephalus, Bucephala, 94
Buddha = Siddhārtha Gautama = Çākyamuni, 22, 66, 67, 161, 173
  his birthplace, 67, 106, 161
  relics of, 141, 158
Buddhism, 66-9; 22, 34, 105
  compared with Brahmanism, 64, 65, 68
  patronised by Açoka, 104
  professed by Çaka satraps, 143
  second council of Vaiçālī, 169
  languages and literature of, 8, 14, 69, 75-6, 81, 105
  its disappearance from the main continent of India, 68, 109
  its retention in Ceylon and Nepal, 108, 109
Burgess, Dr James, 149

ÇAKAS (Scythians), 132, 136-44, 147
  invasion of Bactria, 127; 118, 120
Çaka era, 22, 144, 147
Çaka princes and satraps:
  Kāpiça and Takshaçilā (Gandhāra), 133, 141-2
  Mathurā, 130, 142-3, 174
  Mālava, 143-4
  Surāshṭra, 147
Çākala = Siālkot, 130, 172
Çakasthāna = Seistān, 137-8; 27, 140, 144
Çākya, 66, 161
Çākyamuni, *v.* Buddha
Cambyses, king of Persia, 81
caste-system, 40, 45, 48, 68
Çātakarṇi, 160, 175
Çatapatha Brāhmaṇa, 56-7
Çātavāhana, 160
Caucasus = Hindu Kush = Paropanisus, *q.v.*
Central Asia, 26, 32
Ceylon = Laṅkā or Tāmraparṇī:
  early language and literature, 14-5
  epic poems, 75
  Buddhism, 108-9
chakravartin, 96
Chāṇakya, 103
Chandrabhāgā = Chenāb = Acesines = Asiknī, *q.v.*
Chandragupta, Maurya emperor, 20-1, 100-3
Chandragupta II Vikramāditya, Gupta emperor, 115
Charmaṇvatī = Chambal, 162
Chautang = Dṛishadvatī, 47, 51
Chedi, 162
  era, 22
Chenāb = Chandrabhāgā = Acesines = Asiknī, *q.v.*
Chera = Kerala, 164

China, connexion with India, 25, 28
Chinese Buddhist scriptures, 69
  Buddhist pilgrims, 169, 174
  historians, 8, 127
Chinese Turkestān, 18, 27
Choḷa, 150, 162
Choḷa-maṇḍala = Coromandel, 162
chronology of Ancient India, 16, 21-3, 181-5
  v. also Purāṇas
Chuṭu family of Andhra kings, 160, 175
Çītalā, 158
civilizations, primitive Indian, 28-9, 46
  early Indo-European, 3-5
  Aryan, 8-11, 26, 28-33, 36, 40-6, 47-9
  Dravidian, 9, 26, 28-9
  in Western Asia, 78-80
  in Chinese Turkestān, 27
Claudius, Roman emperor, 90, 162
coin-legends, language of, 13-4
  bilingual, 18-9, 125-6, 152-5
  Brāhmī, 151-2, 155
  Kharoshṭhī, 140, 153-5
  Greek, 18-9, 125-6, 140, 152-5
coin-types: Athene, characteristic of the house of Euthydemus, 128-9, 153
  Zeus enthroned, characteristic of the house of Eucratides, 153
  caduceus, 153-4
  chaitya, 152
  dancing girl, Indian, 152
  Dioscuri, caps of, 154
  elephant, head of, 153-4
  Kāpiça, tutelary deity of, 133
  lion, maneless, 152
  steel-yard, 151
  symbols, punch-marked, 151
  tree within railing, 155
  trident battle-axe, 155
  Viçvāmitra, 154
coins as sources of history, 8, 17, 19
  ancient Indian, 13-4, 151-2, 173
  Græco-Bactrian, 125
  Græco-Indian, 18-9, 123, 125-6, 128-30, 140, 143, 153-5
  Çaka, 140-4, 154
  Pahlava, 138-9, 144-6
  Parthian, 126
  Roman in S. India, 162
communities, oligarchical or self-governing, 55, 77
comparative philology of Indo-European languages, 2-6
conquests, nature of Indian, 96-7
coronation ceremonies in Aitareya Brāhmaṇa, 54
çramaṇa, 57
Çrāvastī, 173, 175
Crœsus, king of Lydia, 86
Crooke, Mr W., 35
çruti, 59
Ctesias, 83; 82, 87, 90
Çūdra caste, 45
Çunaḥçepa, 54
cuneiform alphabet, decipherment of, 82
Çuṅga dynasty, 113-6
Cunningham, Sir A., 156
Çūrasena, 162, 174; 51
Çūrpāraka = Sopāra, 161, 175
Curtius (Q. Curtius Rufus), 90
Cutch, *v.* Kaccha
Çutudrī = Zadadrus or Zaradrus = Sutlej, 162-3
Cyrene, 108
Cyrus, king of Persia, 80-1, 84

DAÇARATHA (1) Maurya king, 110
  (2) father of Rāma, 172
Daimachus, 103-4
Dakshiṇā-patha = Deccan (*dakkhiṇa* = *dakshiṇa* = 'southern'), 31-2, 163
  v. also Southern India
Damayantī, 170
Darius I, king of Persia, 85-6, 127
  inscriptions, 82; 24, 105, 136, 139
Darius II, king of Persia, 83

Darius III Codomannus, king of Persia, 88
Dasyu, 40
Deccan, *v.* Dakshiṇā-patha and Southern India
Delhi, *v.* Indraprastha
Demetrius, Græco-Indian king of the house of Euthydemus, 123-4, 128, 133
  coins, 140, 153
desiccation in Central Asia, 26-7
Devānampiya, 109, 150
Dhānyakaṭaka = Dhāranikotta, 172
Dharaghosha, king of Audumbara, coin of, 154-5
dharma = Pali *dhamma*, 105, 112
Dharmapāla, king ruling at Eran, coin of, 151
Dhṛitarāshṭra, 173
dialects, 13-4
Diodotus, Greek king of Bactria, 118, 120
Dionysius, 104
Dīpavaṃsa, 75
Drangiāna = Seistān (Sijistān), 127, 137-8; 88
Draupadī, 167
Dravidian civilization, 9, 26, 28-9
  languages, 9, 29, 66
Dṛishadvatī = Chautang, 47, 51
Drupada, 167
Dujaka or *Dojaka*, 151
Dyaûs-pitár, 43
dynastic lists, *v.* Purāṇas; Ceylon, epic poems

ēas-t (Eng. *east*), 43
Egypt, 81, 108
English language, Mercian dialect of, 10
Ēōs, 43
epic poems, Sanskrit, *v.* Mahābhārata; Rāmāyaṇa
  their language, 11-2, 72-3
  Pali, 75
Epirus, 108
Eran, coin of, 151
eras, Indian, 21-2
  v. also Çaka era; Vikrama era; Takshaçilā; inscription of Pātika
Eucratides, Bactrian and Græco-Indian king, 124, 126, 133
  house of, 120, 124, 132-4, 140, 146
  coins, 133, 142, 154
Euthydemus, Bactrian and Græco-Indian king, 119-20, 123
  house of, 124-5, 128, 130, 133

Fleet, Dr J. F., 157

Gandhāra, 81-85, 92, 94, 133, 141-2
  Buddhist art, 135
  v. also Kāpiça; Takshaçilā
Gandhāri, 81
Gandharians described by Herodotus, 87
Gaṅgā = Ganges, 163
Ganges and Jumna, the country of = Hindustān, 31-2, 93, 100
Garga, 131-2
Gārgī, 63
Gārgī Saṃhitā, 131-2
Gārgya Bālāki, 62
Garuḍa, 156-7
Gaugamela, 88
Gautama, 57
  v. also Buddha
Gedrosia = N. Baluchistān, 27, 138, 140, 144
genealogies, *v.* Purāṇas; Ceylon, epic poems
geography, Rig-veda, 39, 40
  Yajur-veda, 47
  Çatapatha Brāhmaṇa, 56
  Brahman, Jain, and Buddhist literatures, 77
Girivraja = Rājagṛiha, 109, 166
Girnār = Girinagara, inscribed rock at, 149
Godāvarī, 163
Gomatī = Gumal, 163

Gondopharnes, Pahlava king, 145-6
Gonds, 28
government, different forms of, 55
Græco-Indian kings, *v.* Eucratides, house of; Euthydemus, house of; Yavanas
Greece, Persian expeditions against, 85-7
Greek alphabet in India, 18-9, 125-6, 135, 140
Greeks in India, *v.* Yavanas
Greek writers on Persia, 82-5, 87
Greek and Latin writers on India, 8, 20-1, 24, 89, 90, 93, 95, 100-1, 122
Greek influence on India, 134-5; 132
guild tokens, 151
Gupta era, 22
guru, 59

haoma, 44
Harshavardhana, king of Kanauj, 174
  era, 22
Hastināpura, 165, 173
Hāthigumphā inscription of Khāravela, 116, 160
Heliodorus, Greek ambassador, 134, 157
Hellenic kingdoms, *v.* Bactria; Cyrene; Egypt; Epirus; Macedonia; Parthia; Syria
Hermæus, Græco-Indian king of the house of Eucratides, 133, 146
Herodotus, 83; 24, 82, 84-6, 136
Hesychius of Alexandria, 161
Himālaya = Himavant, 163
Hindu Kush = Paropanisus, *q.v.*
Hindustān = the country of the Ganges and Jumna, 31-2, 93, 100
history, sources of ancient Indian, 6-8, 15-23
  v. also Chinese historians; Chinese Buddhist pilgrims; coins Greek and Latin writers on India; literatures, Indian; inscriptions; seals.
Hittites, 80
Hiuen Tsiang, 169, 174
Horace, 171
Hotar, 46
Hūṇa = Hun, 173
Hydaspes = Jhelum = Vitastā, *q.v.*
Hydraotes = Irāvatī = Rāvi = Parushnī, *q.v.*
Hyphasis = Beās = Vipāç or Vipāçā, *q.v.*

ignis, 42
Imaus, Himaus, or Hemodus = Himavant, 163
'India' = the country of the Indus, 24, 31-2
  province of the Persian empire, 81-8
  reconquered by Alexander the Great, 94-5
  conquered by Yavanas (Græco-Bactrian kings), 123-5
  invaded by Çakas, 136-8, 140, 144
  invaded by Pahlavas, 138-9
  conquered by Kushāṇas, 146
India, the continent:
  names, 24-5
  geographical conformation, 31-2
  primitive inhabitants, 8, 28, 46, 49
  variety of races and languages, 26
  the Dravidians probably invaders, 28-9
  Aryan invaders, 8-9, 40
  relations with the Farther East and with the West in early times, 28, 78, 80
  ancient languages and literatures, 6-16
  political divisions of N. India in the 6th and 5th centuries B.C., 77

the Maurya empire, 99-111
the Kushāṇa empire, 147
the Gupta empire, 166
the Mughal empire, 26, 33, 173
the British dominion, 34
native principalities, 34
common principles of government, 111-2
v. also alphabets; languages; Southern India; and the various headings collected under 'history, sources of ancient Indian'
'Indians' described by Herodotus, 87
Indo-European peoples, 3, 4
religion and mythology, 42-3
social divisions, 45
family of languages, 2-6
v. also languages
Indra, 42, 72, 80
Indraprastha, 173; 26, 47
Indus = Sindhu, 24, 119, 126, 146, 168
inscriptions as sources of history, 8, 17, 19, 21
Persian: Darius, 82; 24, 81, 127, 136, 139
Indian, language of, 13-4
Açoka's inscr. at Girnār, 149-150
Daçaratha's inscrr. in the Nagārjuni Hills, 110
Hāthigumphā inscr. of Khāravela, 116, 160
Besnagar inscr., 134, 156-7
Mathurā Lion-Capital, 142-3, 158
Takshaçilā inscr. of Pātika, 141-2
Ionia, Greek colonies in, 86
Irāvatī = Parushṇī, *q.v.*

JAINISM, 22, 65-6, 69
contrasted with Brahmanism, 64-5, 68
languages and literature of, 8, 14, 66, 69-70, 76-7
patronized by Çaka kings in Mālava, 143
flourished at Mathurā, 174
Janaka, 56-7, 63, 171, 174
Janamejaya, 56-7
Jaxartes = Syr Darya, 127
Jetavana, 173
Jhelum = Hydaspes = Vitastā, *q.v.*
Jina = Vardhamāna Jñātaputra, 65
Jones, Sir William, 2, 6, 20
Jumna = Yamunā, 171
v. also Ganges and Jumna, the country of
Jū-piter, 43
Justin, 122

KĀBUL River = Kubhā, 165
Kābul Valley, 133-4, 140, 142, 146
Kaccha = Cutch, 164
Kāçī = Benares, 164
Kadamba, 160, 175
Kalachuri era, 22
Kali Age, 7
Kālidāsa, 114, 130, 170, 175
Kālikāchāryakathā, 143
Kaliṅga, 164
conquered by Açoka, 106, 116
rise of the later kingdom, 116
Kāmarūpa = Assam, 164
Kāmpilya, 167
Kanarese language, its literary development, 66
Kāñchī = Conjeeveram, 174
Kandahār = Arachosia, *q.v.*
Kanishka, Kushāṇa emperor, 18, 144, 146-7
Kānyakubja = Kanauj, 174
Kāpiça, coins struck at, 133
v. also Çaka princes and satraps
Kapilavastu, 161
karma, 65
Kauçāmbī, 170
Kāverī = Cauvery, 164
Kerala = Chera, 164
Keralaputra, 150, 164
Kharaosta, 158

Khāravela, king of Kaliṅga, 116, 160
Kharoshṭhī alphabet, 17-8
coin-legends, 140, 151-5
inscriptions, 143, 158
'King of Kings,' title used by Persian, Parthian, Çaka, and Pahlava kings, 139
kingdoms of N. India, 77
kingly titles in India, 55
Koṅgu-deça, 164
Kosala = Oudh, 69, 164, 170; 72
coins of, 115
Kṛishṇa, 174
Kṛishṇā (1) = Kistna, 159, 164
(2) = Draupadī, 167
Krivi = Pañchāla, 167
Krumu = Kurram, 165
Kshatriya caste, 45
its literature, 11
its religion, 72
Kshāyathiyānām Kshāyathiya = *Shāhan-shāh*, 139
Kubhā = Kābul River, 165
Kuçanābha, 174
Kujūla Kadphises, 133, 146
Kuṇḍapura = Basukund, 169
Kuru, 50, 165
Kuru-kshetra 47, 51, 173
Kushāṇa conquest of Kābul Valley, 125, 133, 146
conquest of Çakas, 132, 144
empire under Kanishka, 146-7

Lalita-vistara, 17
language, scientific study of, 2-6
preserves the record of early civilization, 4, 5
natural (*prākṛita*), 13-4
artificial or literary (*saṃskṛita*), 9-12
languages, Indo-European family, 2-6
Aryan group, 4, 5, 29-31
Dravidian, 9, 29, 66
Laṅkā = Ceylon, 165
Latin writers, *v.* Greek and Latin writers on India
legends, ancient, 54, 73, 75
Liaka Kusūlaka, Çaka satrap of Takshaçilā, coins of, 140, 142, 154
Licchavi, 169
literary languages, 9-12
literatures, Indian, as sources of history, 6-17
early chronology of, 23
Vedic, 36-9, 44, 46-7, 49
Brāhmaṇas, 52-9
Upanishads, 59-63
Jain, 69, 70, 76-7
Buddhist, 69, 70, 75-7
Sūtras, 76-7
Brahman epics, 70-3
Purāṇas, 73-5
Buddhist epics, 75-6
Classical Sanskrit, 10-2, 14-5, 130-2
local government in India, 96, 111
Lumbini-vana, 106, 161

Macedonia, 108
Madhya-deça, 'the Middle Country,' 50
Madhyamikā = Nāgarī, 131
Magadha = S. Bihār, 165-6; 33, 77, 93, 100, 110-1, 114, 170
Magas, king of Cyrene, 21
Mahābhārata, 70-3; 11, 47, 51, 57
Mahābhāshya, 131
Mahānadī, 164, 166
Mahārāshṭra, 166
Mahāsena, king of Ceylon, 75
Mahavaṃsa, 75
Mahāvīra = Vardhamāna Jñātaputra, 65
Mahendra = Mahinda, 75, 109
Maitreyī, 63
Mālava (1) = Mālwā, 166; 144, 170
(2) = Mālaya or Malaya = Malli, 166
Mālavikāgnimitra, 114, 130, 170
Manu, Laws of, 50, 96
Marcus Aurelius, Roman emperor 90
Marshall, Dr J. H., 156

Maru, 166
Māthava, 56
Mathurā = Muttra, 174
  Hindu princes, 143, 174
  under Greek kings, 131
  Çaka satraps, 142-3
  under Kushāṇas, 174
  the Lion-Capital, 142, 158
Matsya, 50-1, 166-7
Maues = Moa = Moga, Çaka king, 141
  family of, 144-5
  coins, 140, 154
  inscription, 141
Maurya empire, 99-112; 20, 33, 121
  its relations with Hellenic kingdoms, 101-2, 104, 108
  its extent, 106-8, 118
  governed by viceroys, 108
  its decline, 110, 113-4, 116-8, 122
Max Müller, Prof. F., 29
Megasthenes, 102-3; 90
Menander = Milinda, Græco-Indian king of the house of Euthydemus, 128-31
  coin, 153
Mercian dialect of English, 10
Middle Country = Madhya-deça, *q.v.*
migration of peoples, 26
Mihirakula, Hūṇa king, 173
Milinda = Menander, *q.v.*
Milinda-Pañha, 129-30
Mitanni, kings of, 80
Mithilā, 171, 174
Mithradates I, king of Parthia, 119, 124, 126, 139, 142
Mithradates II the Great, king of Parthia, 138-9
Mitra, 80
Moabite stone, 18
Moga = Moa = Maues, *q.v.*
Mongolian races and languages, 26
Mudrā-rākshasa, 100, 103
Mughal empire, 26, 33, 173
Murā, 100
Muttra = Mathurā, *q.v.*

Nādir Shāh of Persia, 26
Naksh-i-Rustam, inscriptions of Darius at, 82, 84
Nala, 167
Nanda dynasty, 100
Nandasi-Akasā, 158
nandi-pada, 152
Narmadā = Narbadā, 167
Nearchus, 94
Negamā, 151
Nicaea, 94
Nirukta, 11, 38
Nishadha, 167
nomes or fiscal units of the Persian empire, 83, 85
North-western region of India, 31-32, 117-8

Old Persian language, 82, 84
Orosius, 126

pada-pāṭha, 38
Pahlava (Parthian) invaders of India, 136, 138-40, 144-6
Pali language, 14-5
  Buddhist literature, 69, 75, 105
Pallava, 167
Pañchāla = Krivi, 47, 51, 131, 167
Pañchāla, N., 167
  coins, 115
Pañchāla, S., 167
Pāṇḍu, 71, 173
Pāṇḍya, 150, 167-8
Pāṇini, 131
Pantaleon, Bactrian and Græco-Indian king of the house of Euthydemus, coin of, 152
Paropanisadae = Paruparaesanna, 84, 88, 168
Paropanisus or Paropamisus = Hindu Kush, 84, 89, 140, 168
Parthia, Hellenic kingdom, 118-9, 142
  Çaka invasion, 127, 137
  Pahlavas and Çakas hold the eastern provinces, 138-9

Parushṇī = Irāvatī = Hydraotes = Rāvi, 168; 93
Pāṭaliputra = Patna, 102-3, 174; 115, 131, 170
Patañjali, 131
Pātika, Çaka satrap of Takshaçilā, 141-2
Paurava = Porus, Indian king, 92, 96
Periplus maris Erythræi, 129
Persepolis, inscriptions of Darius at, 82, 84
Persia, connexion with India, 25-6, 28, 81, 88, 140
Persian (Achæmenid) empire, 80
  subject peoples in inscriptions of Darius, 82
  nomes or fiscal units, 83, 85
  dominions in India, 81-8, 123-4
  expeditions against Greece, 85-7
Persian influence on India, 26, 82, 142, 156
Persian religion, ancient, 43-4
philology, comparative, of Indo-European languages, 2-6
Photius, 83
Phraates II, king of Parthia, 137
pippali = peperi = pepper, 162
Pliny, 159
portraits on Bactrian coins, 120
Porus = Paurava, Indian king, 92, 96
Prāchyāḥ = Prasioi, *q.v.*
præfectus, 45
Prakrit, 13-4
  coin-legends, 18-9, 125-6, 140
Prasioi = *Prāchyāḥ*, the 'Easterns' = the peoples of the country of the Ganges and Jumna (Hindustān), 93, 100
Pratishṭhāna = Paithan, 174-5
Prayāga, 175
primitive inhabitants of India, 8, 28, 46, 49
  religious beliefs and social institutions, 35, 49
prose literature, development of, 52-3
  early, 56
Ptolemy Philadelphus, king of Egypt, 21, 104
Punjab, *v.* 'India' = the country of the Indus
Purāṇas, 73-5; 70
  Maurya dynasty, 110
  Çuṅga dynasty, 113-4
  Andhra kings (Çātavāhana dynasty), 117, 160
  chronology and dynastic lists, 7, 16-7, 74-5, 114
purohita, 45
Pūru, 92
  v. also Paurava
Pushyamitra, 114, 130, 170

Rājagṛiha = Girivraja, 109, 166
Rājūla or Rājuvula = Rañjubula, Çaka 'Great Satrap':
  coins, 140, 143
  inscr. on Mathurā Lion-Capital, 143, 158
Rāma, hero of the Rāmāyaṇa, 71-2
Rāmāyaṇa, 71-2; 11, 57
Rañjubula = Rājūla, *q.v.*
Rāvi = Irāvatī = Hydraotes = Parushṇī, *q.v.*
Rawlinson, Sir Henry, 82
religion of knowledge, 58-61, 64-5
religion of works, 58-60, 64
religions:
  v. primitive inhabitants of India;
  Persian religion, ancient;
  Rig-veda; Yajur-veda; Atharva-veda; Brāhmaṇas; Upanishads; Brahmanism;
  Jainism;
  Buddhism
religious toleration in India, 111-2
Rig-veda, 36-9; 4, 30
  geography, 39, 40, 81
  language, 10, 38
  religion, 42-4

deities worshipped by kings of Mitanni, 80
hymns and metres, 44
social and political conditions, 40-2, 44-6
rivers, Indian, change of courses, 95; 51, 163
mentioned in Rig-veda, 39
Rohiṇī, 161
Rome, trade with S. India, 162
coins found in S. India, 162
Rudradāman, Great Satrap of Surāshṭra and Mālava, 149

SACRIFICE, traces of human, 54
in Rig-veda, 42-3, 44-5
in Yajur-veda, 47-8
Sadānīra, 56, 171
Sāketa, 131, 172
Samataṭa, 168
Sāma-veda, 46
saṃhitā-pāṭha, 38
Sandrokottos = Chandragupta, Maurya emperor, *q.v.*
Sandrophagos = Chandrabhāgā, 161
Sanskrit, the 'discovery' of, 2, 5, 6
varieties of the language, 11-2
the sacred language of Brahmanism, 14, 69
used also by Jains and Buddhists, 15
Vedic, 10, 38
Brāhmaṇa, 11, 55-6
epic, 11-2, 72-3
classical, 10-2, 14-5, 130-2
Buddhist in Nepāl, 105
Sarasvatī = Sarsūti, 47, 51
Satiyaputra, 150
satraps, government by, 141
appointed by Alexander, 95-6
Saubhūti = Sophytes, coin of, 151-2
Sāyaṇa, 39
Scylax, 84, 94
Scythian races and languages, 26
Scythians, *v.* Çakas
seals, as sources of history, 8, 19
Seistān = Çakasthāna, 137-8; 27, 140, 144
Seleucus Nicator, king of Syria, invasion of the Punjab, 101; 20, 98, 120-1
Shāhan-shāh, 139
Shakespeare, 170
Siālkot = Çākala, 130, 172
Siddhārtha Gautama = Buddha, *q.v.*
Sijis ān = Seistān, *q.v.*
Sind = 'India,' the country of the Indus, *q.v.*
Sindhu = Indus, 24, 119, 126, 146, 168
Sītā, heroine of the Rāmāyaṇa, 72, 171, 174
Skandagupta, Gupta emperor, 149
Skeat, Prof., 10
Smith, Mr V. A., 103
smṛiti, 59
Sogdiāna = Bukhāra, conquered by Alexander, 89
invaded by Yueh-chi, 127-8
soma, 43
Sophytes = Saubhūti, coin of, 151-2
Southern India, 31-2
history of, 9
Tamil kingdoms mentioned in Açoka's inscriptions, 107, 150
Dravidian languages, 9, 29, 66
Spalirises, Pahlava king, 144
Stein, Sir Aurel, 27
Strabo, 104, 122, 129-30
Strato I Soter, reigning conjointly with his grandson,
Strato II Philopator, Græco-Indian kings of the house of Euthydemus, coins of, 129-130, 140, 143
stūpa = tope, 115, 158, 172-3
Subhagasena = Sophagasenus, 121
Sudās, 168
Sumerian civilization, 79
Surāshṭra, 168-9
Çaka kings of, 147
Susian language, 82, 84

Sūtras, 76-7; 53
Suvarṇagiri, 109
Suvāstu = Swāt, 169
svarāj, 55
Syria, Seleucid kingdom of, 101, 119
revolts of Bactria and Parthia, 118-9
relations with the Maurya empire, 101-2, 108

TAKSHAÇILĀ = Taxila, 92, 175
Alexander the Great, 92, 96
Græco-Indian kings, 133, 157
Çaka satraps, 133, 140-3, 154
copperplate inscription of Pātika, 141
Tamil kingdoms in Açoka's inscriptions, 107, 150
language, literary development of, 66
Tāmraparṇī (1) = Tambapaṇṇi = Ceylon, 107, 169
(2) = Tāmbraparṇi, 169
Tāṇḍya Brāhmaṇa, 55
Tāpī = Tāpti, 169
Taxila = Takshaçilā, *q.v.*
Thomas, Dr F. W., 158
Thomas, St, 145
Tibetan Buddhist scriptures, 69
Tissa, king of Ceylon, 109
Tīw: *Tīwes-dæg* = *Tuesday*, 43
tope = *stūpa*, 115, 158, 172-3
Toramāṇa, Hūṇa king, 173
Traikūṭaka era, 22
Trogus, 122

UDGĀTAR, 46
Udumbara, 154-5
Ujjayinī = Ujjain, 143, 175
upanishad, 53
Upanishads, 58-63; 72, 76, 81
Ushāsa, 43

VAIÇĀLĪ, 169
Vaiçya caste, 45
Vaijayantī = Baṇavāsi, 175
Vālmīki, 72
vaṃçānucharita, 74
Vaṅga = Bengal, 170
Vardhamāna Jñātaputra = Jina = Mahāvīra, 65; 22, 169
varṇa, 45
Varuṇa, 54, 80
Vasumitra, 114, 130
Vaṭasvaka, 152
Vatsa, 170
veda, 36
Vedas, *v.* Rig-veda; Sāma-veda; Yajur-veda; Atharva-veda
Vedānta, 62
Venis, Prof., 157
Viçvāmitra, figure of, *v.* coin-types
Vidarbha, 114, 170
Videha = Videgha, 56, 69, 170-1
video, 36
vidhi, 53
Vidiçā = Bhīlsa, 115, 166
Vikrama era, 22
Vikramāditya (1) = a king of Ujjain, 143
(2) = Chandragupta II, Gupta emperor, 115
village communities, 111
Vindhya, 171; 50
Vipāç or Vipāçā = Hyphasis = Beās, 93, 130, 171
Virgil, 171
Vishṇu, 134, 156-7
Vitastā = Hydaspes = Jhelum, 171; 92, 126
Vonones, Pahlava king, family of, 139, 144-5
vrātya-stoma, 55
Vṛiji, 169

Weber, Prof. A., 55
Western Asia, early civilizations of, 78-80
connexion with India, 80-1
Wima Kadphises, Kushāṇa king, 146
wit-an (cf. Eng. *wit*, *wisdom*, etc.), 36

XERXES I, king of Persia, expedition against Greece, 85-6

YĀJÑAVALKYA, 63
Yajur-veda, 46, 52
  geography, 47
  religious and social conditions, 47-9
Yamunā = Jumna, 171
Yāska, 11, 38
Yaunā 'Ionians' = *Yavana*, *Yona*, 86
Yavanas, Yonas = Bactrian and Indian Greeks:
  mentioned in inscriptions of Darius, 86
  in Indian literature and inscriptions, 86
  two chief royal houses in Bactria and India, 124
  transference of rule from Bactria to India, 125
  conflict with Çuṅga dynasty, 130-1; 114
  conquered by Çakas and Kushāṇas, 132-3, 146
  influence in India, 134-5
  absorbed in the Indian social system, 134-5, 157
Yueh-chi, 127-8, 137

ZADAORUS, Zaradrus = Çutudrī = Sutlej, 163
Zeús patḗr, 43
Zoroaster, 30, 43